Lessons from the Logbook

For Curt –
Thanks for all
the support.
From your friend
Nancy

Library of Congress Cataloging-in Publication Data pending

Fowler, Ron
        Lessons from the logbook, Flying techniques from the best teacher of all: experience.
        1st Ed. February 2000
        ISBN 0-916413-27-6

Cover Photo by Michael Terry/Aviation Legends, Copyright 1999. All rights reserved. Special thanks to 1949 Cessna 195 owner Mike Meloche.
Layout & Design by Steve McGillivray, Sir Speedy Printing 0922, Seattle, WA

Printed in the United States of America by Consolidated Press, Seattle WA 98134

Published by
Aviation Book Company
7201 Perimeter Rd. South, Suite C
Seattle, Washington 98108
Tel: (206) 767-5232
1-800-423-2708
Fax: (206) 767-3428
www.aviationbook.com

Dedication

*To those students
who help me be a better pilot.*

Other books by Ron Fowler:

Flying Precision Maneuvers in Light Airplanes
Preflight Planning
Making Perfect Landings in Light Airplanes
Making Perfect Takeoffs in Light Airplanes
Flying the Private Pilot Flight Test
Flying the Commercial Pilot Flight Test

Lessons from the Logbook

Flying techniques from the best teacher of all: experience

Ron Fowler

Table of Contents

Part II: Departure

Part III: Enroute

Part V: Recurrent Training

Foreword

Proficiency has a nice ring to it, doesn't it? I think everyone wants to be proficient at whatever they do. Proficiency is a close relative to another word with a nice ring: professionalism.

Professionals need to be proficient for the simple reason that their livelihood depends on the level of their capabilities. Pilots needs to be proficient because their life, the lives of their passengers, and possibly the lives of people on the ground depend on how skillful and knowledgeable they are when they are at the controls of an aircraft.

There are risks associated with flying, just as there are risks associated with everything in life. To minimize these risks, pilots, whether they are high-time professional or low-time private pilots, must continuously work to upgrade their flying skills and bank of aviation knowledge.

Both the military and the airlines spend a great deal of time and money on refresher training for their air crews. As an old jet jockey, I can attest to the rigorous and continuous training provided by the Air Force: simulator training, instrument practice, night flying, low level navigation, gunnery training (not recommended for civilians), escape and evasion, deep sea survival, jungle survival, altitude chamber exposure, parachute training (never did the real jump), and the list goes on. Every military flight is a training flight —

even those in combat. If you don't keep learning, you may not be around to collect your next month's flight pay.

The civilian pilot has the biannual flight review with an instructor pilot, but the rest of the time, it is up to the individual pilot to maintain his or her proficiency. This latest book by Ron Fowler is an outstanding refresher on the fundamentals and techniques you learned when you were earning your pilot's license. Read it and take it to heart.

As your teachers told you in school, knowledge is power. Know your limitations, know the limitations of your aircraft, and know your Federal Aviation Regulations. And periodically expand those limitations under the supervision of dual instruction. Make every flight a learning experience, make sure you are physically capable of the flight you are planning (no drugs, no alcohol, and plenty of rest), and practice, practice, practice — flying couldn't be a more exciting skill to master!

Donald H. Walter
Lt. Col., USAF (Retired)

Col. Walter received a Bachelor of Science degree in Aeronautical Engineering from the University of Colorado and a Master of Science degree in Astronautical Engineering from the Air Force Institute of Technology. He had a varied Air Force career: flying high performance jet fighters, as well as multi-engine transport aircraft, and completed 145 combat missions on two tours in Vietnam flying F-4s. Following his retirement from the Air Force, he earned his license as an Airframe and Powerplant Mechanic and worked in both fixed-wing and helicopter maintenance, and was active in the homebuilt aircraft movement. He is the author of the book Building Your Own Aircraft: An Introduction. *Col. Walter is a member of the Experimental Aircraft Association, the Air Force Association, and the Retired Officers Association.*

Preface

I'm one of the luckiest pilots alive — the overwhelming majority of my logbook entries are those devoted toward teaching people how to fly, and I feel fortunate to live in this niche of aviation. I say this because, first, it gives opportunity to introduce so many to the sport of flying, which I much enjoy, and to help them share this adventure in excellence and safety.

Second, instructing provides the finest entertainment imaginable, as you watch ordinary people take on new and demanding challenges — and winning. With each win, flight students gain new perspectives of their potentials; of who they are and what they expect of themselves. And in doing so, they elevate themselves far, far above ordinary. I'm sure many carry their new self-expectations, born aloft, into their everyday lives lived aground.

Then, there's the simple fact that students help their instructors learn so much more about flying.

Don't get me wrong. I didn't learn at the expense of my students. I was well trained and informed for the task from those first hours with those first students, and taught them well. But students and rated pilots engaged in additional training ask questions which deserve other than perfunctory answers. Often, these questions begin with Why.

It's these "why's" which often send instructors back to the books to help formulate complete answers for their students. The bits and pieces of textbook facts are put together and blended with experience to reveal the true relationships of forces at work in real-life flying — not just as clinical, textbook versions.

Finally, as an instructor you're constantly in the air, urging maximum performance from student and airplane alike — wishing most of all to see your student succeed. Each hour aloft brings something new; no two students are the same, no two flights alike. You begin each new day of your livelihood with a clean slate, wondering what new challenges will arise — I'd recommend a flight instructor's life to anyone with a desire to teach and a love for the sky.

The chapters of this book began as articles I wrote in recent years for *Plane & Pilot Magazine* and I thank executive publisher Steve Werner for allowing their use herein.

When I write, I have a particular student or pilot in mind. And in my mind, we converse. The student or pilot asks questions and my answers become the copy. Thus, the material you read is in every sense a collaboration of student and instructor.

It's the hope of this book to bring you into these conversations — first as you read along, then in the cockpit — as you become your own best flight instructor answering your own "why's," filling your own logbook pages with entries of real-life solutions for real-life flying.

Prolog

Flying is one of the few endeavors left to us in which we're allowed to act as total masters of our own welfare. Once aloft, the battery of experts remain behind. It's solely up to the pilot in command to weigh the risk, evaluate the options, command the decision, and preserve the integrity of the flight for passengers and pilot alike. It *is* a heavy responsibility and pilots would have it no other way.

Part I

Preflight

In the last analysis, when the margin is close,
when all the known factors have been considered,
after equations have produced their final lifeless numbers,
one measures a field with an eye, and checks the answer
beyond the conscious mind.

Charles A. Lindbergh, *The Spirit of St. Louis*

Chapter 1

Total Awareness and Colors of the Mind

Simply put, **total awareness** means never being caught by surprise in the cockpit. It is a concept most pilots have heard about, but not experienced. The majority of pilots who never attain total awareness let it elude them simply because they do not understand its simplicity. They feel it is only "theory stuff," yet it is a real and very visible tool — a pilot's seemingly sixth sense, which elevates the professionally-minded flier above the ordinary.

A certain pilot comes to mind when I think about total awareness and professionalism. The student had soloed two weeks earlier and was preplanning a dual cross-country flight. She finished her inquiries, calculations, and preparations so we headed for the airplane.

"Shouldn't be a bad crosswind when we land," she said.

"OK... why do you say that?" I asked.

"Well," she said, "flight service gave the wind there as 30° at 12 knots; the *Airport/Facility Directory* shows the runway 350°. The airplane flight manual says the plane can take an 18-knot direct crosswind, and we've already landed with a 10-knot component."

"Sounds great," I said. She had put together available information and evaluated it against her plane's ability as well as her own skill. She knew what she would likely face on landing even before we took off.

"Besides," she added, grinning, "if the wind does kick up, there's an airport eight miles beyond with three runways. OK, Teach?"

She had planned a possible "out." Inexperienced in hours, maybe, but certainly experienced in a good flying awareness with her mind in the "green."

Your total awareness stems from three primary sources: abundant aeronautical knowledge, adequate preflight planning, and a constant observation aloft.

Aeronautical Knowledge

Total awareness begins with knowledge, and in flying there is so much to learn. Just because you once passed a written test does not mean you've finished your studies; it only means you've satisfied minimum government standards. Stay a student of the art. Study each article and book you discover having significance to the type of flying you conduct.

If you asked me to list just three basic texts to read, study, and fully understand, I'd include:

1. Aviation Weather (US Government Printing Office publication). Weather is the stage upon which our flight plays across. You need to know its changing character. A good understanding of this book will make you more weather-wise than the average meteorologist giving forecasts on the evening news.

2. Aeronautical Information Manual (US Government Printing Office publication). Our lives aloft are directed by standard operating procedures. This publication is a concise, explicit guide to these procedures — from preflight activities, to communications, airport operations, and beyond. It is well indexed. If there is **any** procedure that confounds you, you will likely find the solution here.

3. Airplane Operating Manual (AFM) or *Pilot's Operating Handbook (POH)* for the plane you fly. There is no such thing as a "forgiving airplane." All planes have operating limits in terms of airspeeds, aerodynamic forces, loading, and performance. Particularly in light planes, the parameters of these limits are quite narrow. Operate the plane within these limits and it will behave and perform as expected. Try to operate *beyond* these design limits, however, and *no one* knows what to expect. You suddenly become a test pilot engaged in on-the-job training. The manufacturer's recommended procedures for specific flight situations are stated with the prime intent to keep you within the plane's design limitations.

The quest for aeronautical knowledge is a never-ending effort. Any pilot would be wise to apply a rule of thumb: set aside one evening a week for continuing study.

Preflight Planning

Total awareness depends upon gathering the facts of the flight before departure. For as many years as I can remember, the FAA has listed "inadequate preflight planning" as the number one reason for aircraft accidents. Accordingly, the success of your flight is largely determined before your wheels even leave the ground. Let your research follow the format of total preflight planning: the environment, the airplane, the pilot.

The Environment

Basically, environmental elements of awareness that effect a flight fall into four categories: departure and arrival, en route, communications, and traffic movement.

Departure and Arrival

Aware pilots understand how four environmental factors influence their plane's takeoff and landing performance:

1. Runway surface. As a rule of thumb, unpaved runways add about 20% to distances charted in the AFM for paved surfaces; 30% if the grass needs mowing or is wet.

2. Field elevation. Each 1,000 feet of field elevation requires about 10% additional takeoff distance and about 5% extra on landing.

3. Field temperature. As a rule of thumb, each 25°F above standard temperature for the field elevation adds about 10% takeoff distance and decreases rate of climbout by the same percent. (Figure "standard temperature" as 60°F at sea level; decrease by 3° for each 1,000 foot field elevation.)

4. Surface wind. In general, light planes require about 20% less takeoff and landing distances for each 10 knots of direct headwind.

En route

Environmental factors that must be part of your awareness en route include:

1. Obstacles and terrain. Study your sectional chart closely and "red pencil" any obstacle or terrain within 5 miles of your route that rises within 1,000 feet of your planned cruising altitude (2,000 feet in mountain areas where rising terrain comes very quickly to planes with a sluggish rate of climb).

2. Alternate airports. Be aware of the closest *paved* airport along each 100 mile segment of your route. Unpaved airports are too hard to find when you need them. For the same reason, select airports with beacons for night flight.

3. Route mid-point. Calculate your mid-point ETA and mark it on your sectional chart. An awareness of gaining journey's mid-way gives a time and place for review; adjustment of destination ETA, evaluation of fuel needs, revision to filed flight plan and the like... a time, perhaps, to munch an apple.

4. Expected visibilities. Be aware of the hazards associated with reduced visibility, as you receive your weather briefing:

    a. Weather ahead and around is often hidden. You can fly right into it before you can see and avoid.

    b. Navigation becomes difficult. Chances increase for getting lost, with associated fuel concerns.

    c. Disorientation is possible, particularly with a fatigued or anxious pilot.

    d. Chances increase for collision, particularly as you descend toward your destination; rising terrain, obstacles, or traffic.

5. Extent of cloud cover. A VFR pilot is wise not to over-fly a cloud layer that exceeds the weather briefer's term "scattered." And once above an acceptable layer, an aware pilot will descend well before the clouds cover more than a quarter of the terrain below. Aware pilots recognize the hazards:

    a. Scattered bases can close up quickly. Once trapped above, without ample terrain in sight, there is strong likelihood of getting lost.

    b. Once vertical development begins, clouds can out-climb light aircraft and often exceed the plane's service ceiling.

    c. Once lateral development begins, a cloud deck can easily outrange the plane's remaining fuel.

6. Extent of precip. Aware pilots know it is difficult to dodge between showers of precip that exceed a forecast's "widely scattered," which is up to 25% terrain coverage. The precip areas just move around too much to stay out of them. "Isolated" thunderstorms need at least 10 miles clearance.

7. Turbulence. Aware pilots have learned through painful experiences that passengers will not tolerate more than the briefer's "moderate" turbulence, defined as changes in altitude and attitude. Passengers will feel strains against their seatbelts and loose objects in the cockpit will move about.

8. Winds aloft. Know the winds aloft so you can select the cruising altitude most advantageous to your flight. These known

FLIGHT LOG

From _____ to _____ (Alternate AP: _____)

Wind Aloft @ _____ MSL: _____ deg. @ _____ kts.

True Airspeed @ Altitude: _____ kts.

True Course: _____ deg.

Wind Correction Angle: +/- _____ deg.

True Heading: _____ deg.

Ground Speed: _____ kts.

Magnetic Variation: +/- _____ deg.

Magnetic Heading: _____ deg.

Compass Deviation: +/-_____ deg.

Compass Heading to Destination: _____ deg.

Distance to Destination: _____ n.m.

Time to Destination:_____ : _____ hrs./min.

Fuel Flow @ Altitude: _____ gal./hr.   Gal. aboard: _____

Endurance with Reserve: _____ : _____ hrs./min.

ETD _____ :   _____ ETA _____ : ____

Figure 1-1
A calculated flight plan brings awareness of time, distance, situation and position to the pilot. Flights anticipating a significant wind shift en route will require secondary estimates from that point forward.

winds also allow you to correlate gathered information into a simple flight log (see Figure 1-1). Aware pilots compile a flight log. Doing so takes guesswork out of the flight.

Communications

A cross-country is rich in an environment of services which contribute safety, efficiency, and convenience to the flight. You can best make yourself aware of these services by compiling a communications frequency log (see Figure 1-2). Additionally, such a log places all anticipated frequencies at finger-tip convenience; far more practical than trying to find and read them in flight on a bouncing navigation chart. All services and frequencies may be researched from a single, easy-to-use source — the *Airport/ Facility Directory*, available where you purchase charts.

Traffic Movement

Aware pilots anticipate the traffic environment they plan to enter, and evaluate the needs of this environment against their knowledge and experience. We have all witnessed pilots trained and experienced at only non-controlled airports, totally overwhelmed with traffic environments at Class B or C airports. Then, there was opportunity for colossal pilot error. Conversely, we have all dodged pilots familiar with only the protections of controlled airports, totally oblivious to precautions necessary when entering the traffic environment of a non-controlled airport. Pilots unfamiliar with either environment need to gain an awareness of correct procedures. This can be accomplished in two steps. First, a study of the *Aeronautical Information Manual*, Chapter 4: Air Traffic Control. This chapter concisely and clearly states the procedures for using both environments. Step 2 calls for in-flight instruction within the unfamiliar airspace.

COMMUNICATIONS LOG

Facility	Station	Station	Station	Station
ATIS				
AWOS				
FSS				
CLNC. DEL.				
GND. CON.				
TOWER				
DEP. CON.				
APP. CON.				
CENTER				
FLT. WTCH.				
VOR				
NDB				
ILS				
CTAF				
PHONE#	FSS: _____		AWOS: _____	
FSS				
AWOS				

Figure 1-2
All frequencies and phone numbers can be researched before the flight, either from the sectional or Airport/Facility Directory, then reduced to a communications log for in-flight use.

The Airplane

Three areas of awareness surround the operation of an airplane: the plane's physical state, correct pilot procedures for each phase of the flight, and its performance capability.

Physical State

Close adherence to the manufacturer's preflight inspection checklist provides the only assurance that a critical item is not overlooked. If there is a checklist item you do not fully understand, make yourself aware. Ask a mechanic.

Correct Procedures

Different makes and models often require special operating procedures. Manufacturers provide checklists for all anticipated procedures, from engine starting to shutdown. But these lists are often hard to find and use when needed. A suggestion: reduce the flight manual's published checklists to your own best penmanship within a handy-sized notebook.

Performance Capability

Every pilot should own and study a copy of the manual for the plane they fly. Aware pilots do not rely upon guesswork or chance luck when evaluating their plane's performance against needs for the flight. *Any* concern calls for the plane's performance charts. As a rule of thumb, a single-engine pilot should calculate takeoff and landing requirements anytime field elevation exceeds 3,000 feet, temperature tops 85°F, or runway length is under 3,000 feet.

A part of total awareness is that things can go wrong — the headwind dies, faulty brakes, flawed technique, and many others. To your calculated distances, add a 50% margin for safety. Charted cruise performance values of range and speed are valid only if the pilot flies with an accuracy which avoids constant corrections to altitude and heading, employs correct fuel leaning technique, and has loaded the plane properly.

Mishap does not come to all planes loaded incorrectly. It usually takes a stall to trigger the disaster. Some weight and balance charts are difficult to interpret. If you don't know how to use yours, find someone who can show you how. As a rule of thumb, run a weight and balance calculation anytime the seating is over half filled, there is weight in any luggage bay, or extreme aft seats are occupied.

The Pilot

Any particular flight can impose special challenges to a pilot's airmanship. Aware pilots are very cognizant of their knowledge and skill limitations. They do not depend on know-how or skill which logic tells them they cannot deliver. Here is a good rule to follow: obtain further instruction in any phase of airmanship which vexes you — crosswinds, navigation, communications, basic skills of altitude, heading and airspeed control, and the like. Awareness is a process of never-ending education.

Colors of the Mind

Total awareness aloft is dependent upon keen observations of a ready mind. The mind's readiness is subject to the pilot's will. The pilot must decide if the mind is to work-in its white, green, or red zone.

White Zone

At one time or another, we have all experienced our mind's white zone. Have you ever driven to work, parked your car, then realized you could not recall details of the drive? If so, your mind was in its white zone — at wander and oblivious to situations. If a need for quick action arose, your mind would first need to return to the job at hand — driving the car — then evaluate the situation, then decide upon options, and still have enough time to take action. Aloft, pilots can allow their minds to enter the white zone if they become preoccupied with business, plans, or worries that belong on the ground. A mind befuddled with sorting out facts of the flight that should have been settled by preflight planning is a common example of a mind in the white. Keen observation and quick actions are doubtful.

Green Zone

When in its green zone, your mind is supplied with facts of the flight and focused on the job at hand. Your actions are filled with the satisfying enjoyment of flying accurate altitudes, headings and airspeeds. You maintain a constant awareness of position, stay abreast of weather ahead and around, keep your alternate airports in mind, tend to already-anticipated communications, and maintain traffic vigilance.

You are aware your flight is normal and progressing according to plan. Yet, you remain aware to the fact that things can go wrong, and are alert for the first hint of trouble. In short, you are totally aware of the flight's needs, your airplane, and your surroundings.

Red Zone

At the first hint of concern your already-alert and informed mind is ready to jump into its red zone. You are in good position to quickly identify the problem, weigh the risks, and select your best possible options.

Total awareness, then, is not just "theory stuff." It is the result of a pilot's personal decision to acquire abundant aeronautical knowledge, adequately plan the flight, and maintain constant observations aloft that play across the colors of the mind.

Chapter 2

Destination Known

Plan a flight through a region of the sky you haven't yet voyaged to a port you don't yet know. Go alone, but be prepared. During these solitary moments, you can see things the way you want to see things, free from the interference of others' suggestions and agendas. It is quality time to reflect on happenings past, evaluate the here and now, and lay plans for what you wish yet to come.

Too often we find ourselves caught up in a circus balancing act driven by ever-quickening marches of responsibilities in our life's three rings: providing a living, family demands, community needs. But a life consumed by others soon has only a burnt-out soul of ashes, able to help no one. In our intense society, complications and demands often deny you a measure of time for yourself. Chances for individual thought — either personal or business — seem to evaporate before the day is done; your own goals abandoned even before they're fully identified.

But aloft! As a pilot, you expect to spend and enjoy many hours, quite alone, within the cockpit. Morning flight might pass with only the company of quilted farmlands drifting below. Afternoon may find the companionship of building cumulus. And the mystique of night flight might be shared with the sociability of glowing instruments, while the shimmering planet held centered in the windscreen beckons a more likely destination than the winking beacon ahead and below.

A time and place, surely, for solo thinking. A time and place of sanctuary that gives moments you can exercise creative, undisturbed thoughts that give birth to ideas of merit. That is why I say: plan a flight through a part of the sky you haven't yet flown to a port you don't yet know — and go alone.

Preflighting the Destination Arrival

When flying to a new or distant destination, every argument leads to a need for preflighting your arrival landing before your wheels ever leave the ground. That is to say, make your destination known.

For as many years as I can remember, the FAA has repeated these two facts: inadequate preflight planning continues to lead as the number-one cause for flying accidents; and the landing is the leading time and place for these accidents to occur. There is a definite link between these two facts. The surprise of unexpected situations and conditions at the destination airport can confuse a pilot at the time of a flight's heaviest workload — arrival. And confusion is often a prelude to mishap.

However, all the information necessary to prevent landing surprises is available prior to departure. But these facts are in scattered pieces. It takes preflight research to correlate the useful information from easily accessible sources (see Figure 2-1). Here are a few items to consider:

Crosswind Challenge

For sheer excitement, there are few moments in flying equal to an arriving pilot surprised by a crosswind that exceeds personal skill or aircraft capability. Picture your view through the windscreen of an airplane at odd angles to the centerline and drifting toward runway's edge. Outside the slewing cabin, tires hit with squalling rubber — an occurrence that sends squirts of adrenaline right out your ears.

**Destination Data from Weather Briefing
and Airport/Facility Directory**

• Surface Wind Expected @ ETA: _____ deg. @ _____ kts.

• Runway Headings Available: _____ deg.

• Expected Wind Components (wind favored runway):

   XWND _____ Kts   HWND _____ kts

• Length Wind Favored Runway: _____ ft.

• Runway Surface: _____ paved _____ unpaved

• Field Elevation: _____ MSL

• Expected ETA Temperature: _____ deg.

• Expected Density Altitude: _____ ft.

• Required Runway Length *(including safety margin)*: _____ ft.

• Lighting Available:

   Runway lights: _____ Edge _____ REIL _____ ALS

   Part-time light hours: _____ to _____

   Pilot-activated lights frequency: _____ Mhz

   Rotating beacon: _____ yes _____ no

   Nearby beaconed airport: _____

Figure 2-1
*Compile the information you glean from your preflight preparation into a single form
for quick reference.*

Crosswinds that exceed pilot skill or aircraft capability continue as a major producer of landing accidents. True, people aren't usually injured, but a tattered wing-tip is expensive. And a side-load that collapses a gear to let the prop hit with sudden stoppage brings the price up to a second mortgage.

Estimating ETA Crosswinds

It's very easy to estimate ETA crosswinds before departure. First, simply ask your weather briefer for the surface wind expected at ETA. Second, compare that wind's angle to the runway heading as stated in your *Airport/Facility Directory*. Then, calculate your expected crosswind component with your flight computer or a crosswind component chart (see Figure 2-2). You may also apply three rules of thumb:

1. If the wind is expected to lie within 30° of runway alignment, estimate the crosswind component at half the wind's velocity.

2. If the wind is expected to lie from 30 to 60° across the runway, estimate the component at three-quarters of the wind's velocity.

3. If the wind is expected to lie from 60 to 90° across the runway, estimate the component at the wind's full velocity.

Next, check your airplane flight manual to make certain the expected crosswind doesn't exceed the manufacturer's operational limitations. If your manual doesn't state this value, apply this rule of thumb: don't attempt a landing when the crosswind component exceeds one-third the plane's stall speed.

Finally, relate the expected crosswind component to your personal skill and don't attempt an arrival that exceeds your own demonstrated capability. If the winds are expected to blow on the edge of safety and your destination offers only a single runway, the solution is simple: look to your sectional chart for a nearby

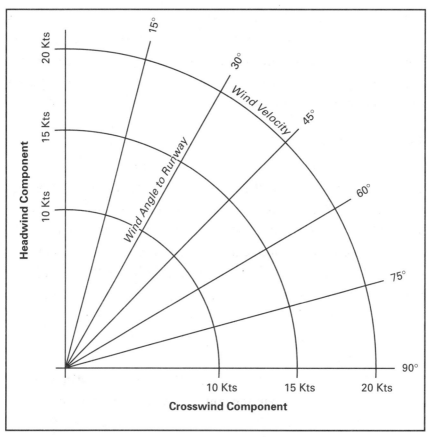

Figure 2-2
Calculate your ETA crosswinds before your wheels leave the ground to avoid surprises at the destination.

alternate with multiple runways. Then, if necessary, you can land there and wait for the wind to shift or subside.

Adequate Runway Length

FAR §91.103 requires that each pilot — before departure — weigh expected landing conditions against the plane's landing performance chart. There are several factors to research and consider.

Runway Length

Your sectional chart states the length of only the longest runway. That may or may not be the wind-favored runway. Look to your *Airport/Facility Directory* for the runway's length that your weather briefing suggests might be the one you will use. Once you have determined runway length available, several factors will dictate whether or not that length is adequate.

Runway Surface

The *Airport/Facility Directory* states the landing surface for each runway at your destination. Some aircraft manuals state only the distance required for a paved braking surface. As a rule of thumb, add 20% to the paved distance for dry grass or turf; 40% if the weather briefing suggests the surface is going to be wet.

Headwind Component

Each 10 knots of headwind generally shortens the no-wind landing distance by 20% for most light aircraft. To estimate your expected headwind component, compare the predicted surface wind at ETA to the runway heading stated in the *Airport/ Facility Directory*. (In areas of large magnetic variation, remember that winds are predicted as "true" while runway headings are stated as "magnetic.")

Then apply the wind's angle with the runway to your flight computer or headwind component chart. You can also estimate the component with three rules of thumb:

1. If the wind is predicted within 30° of runway alignment, figure a headwind component at three-quarters of the wind's forecast velocity.
2. Allow half the wind's velocity as your expected component when the wind's runway angle is predicted from 30 to 60°.

3. When that angle is predicted to exceed 60°, count the headwind as zero.

Field Elevation

Both the sectional chart and the *Airport/Facility Directory* provide field elevation at the destination. Fly your approach at the manufacturer's recommended indicated airspeed, regardless of field elevation. Your true airspeed is, of course, somewhat higher at the higher elevations. This results in a greater groundspeed at touchdown and, hence, a longer ground roll. If your airplane's landing chart doesn't include various elevations, use this rule of thumb: increase the sea-level landing distance by 5% for each 1,000 feet of elevation.

Remember that very high elevation landings (over 5,000 feet) call for a leaned mixture on final to make a needed go-around possible.

Temperature

In the absence of manual information, use this rule of thumb: add 10% of the landing distance for each 40°F predicted above standard temperature for the field's elevation. Standard temperature is 59°F at sea level and decreases about 10°F for each 2,500 feet. (Also, FSS will gladly compute density altitude for any pilot who asks.)

Margin for Safety

Aircraft landing charts usually express required landing distance in two forms: ground roll and total-to-clear obstacle. Ground roll is the approximate distance it takes to brake the plane to a stop once it has touched down. The total-to-clear obstacle distance contemplates an approach over a 50-foot obstruction rear runway's end. This distance provides the total needed to descend over the obstacle to a touchdown point and bring the plane to a stop. In reality, this is very nearly like the glidepath we make even when no obstacles exist.

It is this figure — total-to-clear-obstacle — that is of paramount value to the pilot considering the safety of the landing.

Unless the need to land is critical, don't plan a landing to a runway length of less than 150% of the total-to-clear-obstacle distance for the predicted landing conditions. This safety margin is needed to prevent an unexpected over-run caused by the likes of a sudden down-grade near runway's end, faulty brakes, a headwind that decides to die, a too-fast approach or a simple misreading of the landing chart. As an example, consider landing a fully loaded Skyhawk at a sea-level airport on a hot, windless afternoon. The landing chart calls for about 1,600 feet total distance. Unless that runway exceeds 2,400 feet (1,600 x 1.5), don't try it.

Radio Communications

The same guy who prints Bible verses on pinheads typesets the radio frequencies on our sectionals. Each is nearly impossible to find and read in a bouncing cockpit. Result: confusion and keeping your eyes inside the cockpit at time of arrival — not good.

The preflight solution is easy. Every frequency you'll need at the destination airport is defined and listed in the *Airport/Facility Directory*. Simply compile a radio frequency log on a file card for easy, quick reference (see Figure 2-3).

Nighttime Arrivals

At night, we just don't find and see things as easily as we do during the day, and what we do find and see at night often presents confusing clues. By example, distances seem halved and speeds seem slowed. Preflight research will alleviate many of the destination's nighttime difficulties and illusions.

First, look to your sectional chart. You will be better with a beaconed destination. Airports without rotating beacons have years of experience at hiding from night-flying pilots with a need to land. If your proposed destination doesn't offer a beacon, select a nearby alternate that does.

We find and see things easier when we know where to look. Spend some preflight moments studying the light patterns of towns and cities that lie near your destination airport. The ground light patterns shown as yellow areas on your sectional, quite accurately represent the pattern you'll see from altitude and help pinpoint an airport's location.

Before departure, refer to the *Airport/Facility Directory* to determine the airport lighting available to you. The directory will tell you how to turn on pilot-activated lights, advise of part-time lighting or tower operation (such as REIL or ALS), and provide

Destination Radio Frequency Log

Facility	Frequencies Destination	Alternate
FSS	_____	_____
ATIS/AWOS	_____	_____
TOWER	_____	_____
GND CONTROL	_____	_____
UNICOM/CTAF	_____	_____
VOR	_____	_____
ILS	_____	_____

Figure 2-3
A separate log of destination frequencies will help you keep your eyes outside the cockpit, instead of reading the tiny print on sectionals at a critical time of flight.

identifying lights which may help you differentiate your destination from a neighboring airport.

Consult the *Airport/Facility Directory* for the arrival runway width before you depart, to avoid a common night-flight illusion. A runway considerably wider than that familiar strip at your home field may give the illusion you're too low; you may be led into a high approach and overshoot. A narrower-than-familiar runway creates the opposite illusion, and you might fly a dangerously low approach. These illusions, however, don't disturb a pilot who is forewarned and places emphasis on the altimeter during the approach.

Adequate preflight planning to a new or distant destination eliminates much of the surprise and confusion which can occur upon arrival. Your flight will be more enjoyable and safer for the effort.

Epilogue

The cockpit of an airplane offers the most imaginative platform for solitary thought conceivable. Your thoughts aren't walled in — they can fly from horizon to horizon. The front part of your thinking is focused on the job at hand — flying the airplane — certainly. But while you're doing your job, the back of your mind — left on its own — will be silently generating its best. Let the back of your mind carry an old problem that's marking time, or a new dream in want of a plan, to altitude. The solution is waiting there.

Chapter 3

Personal Weather Minimums

Ragged cloud bases hung a leaden 1,800 feet above the small, rural northern Georgia airport. Rays of weak sunshine had tried several times to seep through occasional breaks in the overcast. But the next sweep of cold rain would again darken the glistening tarmac ramp area.

I had been sitting for two hours on the salvaged Volkswagen van bench seat FBOs called "settees." A pilot and his family were also waiting in the airport lounge. They had made a precautionary landing just as weather had closed in. Snatches of conversation had them homeward bound from vacation, with home only another hour's flight southward. The two small sons had kept themselves entertained for a short while, but their fascination of the red candy machine in the corner, the coverless magazines on the table, and the doo-dads in the showcase counter soon waned. The boys began asking about a time for going home. "Why can't Dad fly in the rain?" "Isn't it going to be dark soon?" As the weather-waiting lengthened, the mother looked more and more strained, and for the past hour the father/pilot had spent most of his time standing by the picture window, watching rain drip from the trailing edge of their Mooney's wings.

During a lull in the rattle of rain, a fifth stranger walked up to the pilot and asked the same question: "Still here?" I could almost hear that pilot's common sense snap. He bunched the muscles in his jaw, ran a hand over his face, let go an explosive sigh, and turned to collect his family. That's when I stood up to stick my oar in because I knew he had come to a very, very bad decision.

Recipe for Disaster

Weather is a most important element in flying safety. Statistics bear out this importance: 25% of all general aviation accidents are weather related, and 40% of fatal accidents are due to pilots flying their planes into adverse weather. Failure to gauge the weather in light of one's own training, experience and skill can be a recipe for disaster. Your first line of defense against these weather statistics is to establish, and reduce to writing, your own personal weather minimums — minimums that reflect your own experience and comfort zone. But you cannot let the opinion of others influence your decision of go or no-go, as did that pilot waiting out the weather in a northern Georgia airport.

FAR Minimums vs. Safety

Neither can a pilot rely on the weather minimums of the regulations to provide guidelines for safety. One can witness the fallacy of this assumption enacted at airports across the country on any foggy morning. There will be several flights flying under VFR waiting for the fog to lift. Usually, along about mid-morning, the airport beacon shuts off, signifying the field has just come up to the legal three miles. Immediately, a few small planes will launch, and one has to wonder: are those pilots capable of flying safely in three miles visibility? In most cases the answer is probably no.

Many pilots draw a false sense of security from the FARs. In many instances, their thinking goes something like this: "Surely the FAA wouldn't state the three-miles visibility and 1,000 foot ceiling if they didn't think it was safe for me to use." This is erroneous thinking.

These minimums imposed by regulations rarely offer safe operating procedures for the average VFR flight. It is not the intent of the FAA to do so. The regulations only dictate absolute minimum *legal* values. Pilots must modify these legal minimums to accommodate their own individual experience, skill, and equipment if they are to fly safely. In most in-flight situations, for example, the average VFR pilot cannot operate safely when a scant, but legal, 1,000-foot ceiling exists. Each pilot must establish specific, *personal* weather minimums.

In order to establish your own cross-country minimums, you need to first identify the separate elements of aviation weather and then consider how each affects the safety of your proposed flight. At the least, VFR pilots must consider the minimums they are willing to tackle in terms of reduced visibility, low clouds, extent of precipitation, intensity of turbulence, and strong crosswinds.

Reduced Visibility

Four potential hazards can creep into the cockpit of a cross-country flight when reduced visibility keeps you from seeing far enough through the Plexiglas.

First and foremost, reduced visibility hides any weather that lies ahead and around the airplane. More often than not, pilots who fly into adverse weather do so simply because they cannot see it in time to avoid it. Or, if they do see the darkening ahead, they really do not know which way to detour, with reduced visibility on all sides.

We often hear the comment: "The plane was caught by weather." Well, no plane has ever been caught by weather — it doesn't reach out and make a snatch at a passing airplane. A pilot has to actually *fly* the plane into the weather, and this can easily happen when pilots can't see where they are going.

The second potential hazard is getting lost over unfamiliar terrain, particularly when you cannot see landmarks six or seven miles ahead. And when you are lost, your eyes tend to lock on the chart in your lap, or the ground beneath you, rather than maintaining a watch for traffic. Getting lost also offers a good opportunity to run out of gas.

The third most apparent hazard of flying through restricted visibility is the increased chance for a midair collision as traffic and obstacles blend into the murk. Two aircraft closing at 160 knots, for example, cover five miles of flight visibility in less than 50 seconds. This may not give you time to become aware of the traffic, determine that a collision course is underway, decide which way to duck, take action with the controls, and still have time for your airplane to get out of the way.

Fourth and finally, reduced visibility often leads to disorientation. Visual references are hard to discern when the horizon is partially hidden. What we think we see and what we really see in poor visibility are not always in agreement. Viewed through a veil of precip, for example, a sloping layer of cloud or smoke lying close to the hidden horizon soon has you flying with a wing low. Or should you fly through four miles and haze, then let a light shower hit your dirty windscreen, you may lose most of your visual references.

Knowing the hazards of poor visibility is just the first step in setting your personal visibility minimums for cross-country flying. It is beneficial for a pilot to actually experience reduced visibility – not just imagine it from written words. The best way to do this is to schedule a short cross-country with an experienced flight instructor when the low visibility is a known value. See for yourself what four, five, six, or seven miles visibility actually looks like. Gauge the degree of difficulty and decide for yourself, from practical demonstration, just what minimum visibility you are willing to tackle.

Be sure your personal visibility minimum allows for some further deterioration to occur en route. How do you determine in-flight visibility? Simply compare the farthest visible charted landmark to the mileage your sectional shows between your position and that landmark. For example, if you decide that six miles visibility, along with a forecast for nothing lower en route, meets your comfort level, do not depart with less than seven miles. Then, should the visibility later drop to six miles, you should still have time to head for an alternate en route airport, or detour to a route that FSS suggests has a better view.

Low Clouds

When clouds force a cross-country flight to within 2,000 feet of the ground, the pilot, whether aware of it or not, is in trouble. That pilot has lost two reserves that mean so much to a flier's safety – abundant altitude and plenty of maneuvering room. Further, low clouds can easily push a plane below radio communication and navigation range, only 30 or so miles at 1,000 feet. At the same time, navigating by landmark becomes doubly difficult with the distorted perspective inherent in low-altitude flying.

Not only does low altitude flying complicate navigation, it also increases a pilot's chances of bumping into something hard. Low clouds squeeze all VFR traffic down into a narrow band of airspace. Many of those pilots have their attention focused on charts and landmarks and coping with the difficulties of navigation, and not on seeing airplanes. Flying 1,500 feet AGL or so might provide obstacle clearance if the terrain is flat and free of tall structures, but on many cross-country flights you encounter both ridges and antennas. What may be 1,500 feet of clearance one minute can become impact the next.

As was the case with reduced visibility, make personal experience a part of your decision when you establish the minimum cloud bases you are willing to fly under on cross-country trips. With an instructor or other weather-experienced pilot aboard, set out on a short cross-country when the cloud deck is of a known value that is low enough to plant concern in your mind. Plan this flight with caution — after all, you are setting out in marginal conditions. Then, carefully analyze the weather briefing to assure yourself that the clouds will probably drop no lower. To cover yourself on that "probably," select a training route sprinkled with alternate airports along the way. You will then see first-hand the difficulty of navigating by landmark, avoiding traffic and clearing obstacles when flying beneath low clouds.

As you set your minimum acceptable cloud height, consider a value that lets you clear the cloud base by at least 1,000 feet, as well as at least 2,000 feet above the terrain. True, the regulations require only 500 feet clearance beneath clouds when you fly below 10,000 feet MSL. But if you have ever had the silver-grey belly of an IFR arrival drop through the clouds above you and a mile ahead, you *know* that isn't enough clearance. (This is one of those experiences in life that provide a subject of conversation for weeks.)

In addition, as you arrive at your personal weather minimum for low clouds, be sure to allow a margin for further deterioration while en route cross-country. Allow for conditions that will let you reach an alternate airport.

Extent of Precipitation

Pilots usually have little difficulty picking their way around rain as long as the precip covers less than 25% of the area and the surrounding sky offers good visibility. Add a little more moisture, bring that coverage closer to half, and it becomes very difficult to stay clear of the rain or possible turbulence. The problem is not solely the percentage of land covered; a pilot certainly doesn't take up half the sky with the plane. The problem with navigation around precip is that it rarely stands still for us. Areas of rain can easily move 30 miles an hour. Often, adjacent showers move at different speeds, and their exact direction of travel, also differing, is difficult to tell from the cockpit. So — to use an analogy — given sufficient coverage and movement, pilots may ride a pinball, trying to stay in the clear, waiting for the weather to push them where they do not want to fly.

Navigating through an area of rain activity is a subject often glossed over in student training. A pilot would be smart to go out and experience the problem with a weather-wise instructor aboard and over familiar ground. Consult with FSS just before your training flight so you know the coverage and compare the weather briefer's terms of coverage with what you see through the windscreen. Then decide after the flight the extent of coverage you would feel comfortable with, and make that value your personal weather minimum for precip.

Turbulence Intensity

Pilots think of turbulence in terms of passenger discomfort, aircraft control, and (gulp) structural damage. It doesn't take much bouncing to discomfort most passengers. The intensity reported as *light* or *moderate* is usually enough to do the job. If the passengers should become, ah ... err ... umm ... discomforted, then be forewarned that they hold a terrible sword of retribution. So if the flight looks choppy, suggest the passengers take a motion-sickness tablet before climbing aboard.

When turbulence is reported as *severe*, you can expect to have trouble keeping the plane under positive control. It causes large changes in airspeed, altitude and heading. While this in itself may not be dangerous at altitude, a pilot's real concern is knowing that severe turbulence is normally punctuated with blasts of extreme turbulence.

Turbulence reported as *extreme* is another matter. The criteria for this reported intensity makes it likely there will be structural damage, and an airplane that is violently tossed about is practically impossible to control. The unfortunate pilot who flies into extreme turbulence will hear the price the plane is paying in pops, groans, and snaps. That pilot will have decided, even before landing, that it is now time to trade it in on a newer one.

As you compare reported intensities to your willingness to accept them, keep in mind that wind rarely blows constant. Light turbulence is often punctuated by puffs of moderate; moderate turbulence with gusts of severe; severe by blasts of extreme.

Strong Crosswinds

The botched crosswind landing is one of the leading causes of aircraft accidents. Not many people get hurt, but airplanes do, and a tattered wing-tip is expensive to replace. If the crosswind touchdown is rough enough to collapse a gear and put the prop into the pavement, the resulting pilot error may cost the price of a new Ford.

A flier's ability to safely handle a particular crosswind component depends primarily on two factors: pilot skill and aircraft capability. The ability to land safely in a crosswind is a pilot skill which can quickly erode. There are two reasons for this. The crosswind maneuver is a complex maneuver. Few maneuvers match it in terms of timing and coordination. Maintaining this skill means constantly using it. Yet the pilot does not often put this skill to its maximum use; the pilot wisely keeps it on the ground when winds are high. As a result, many pilots have a problem with handling significant crosswinds. One rule says use it or lose it. Another rule says don't use it when it will do the most good: when it tests your skill.

The most practical solution to this dilemma lies in on-going, dual instruction. When you look out the window and the wind is blowing harder than you would want to land in, call your favorite instructor for an on-the-spot schedule. Then, with the instructor aboard, sharpen your skill and determine your comfortable, personal crosswind limitation. The prudent pilot conducts this recurrent training flight every few months. It is the best insurance a flier can buy against a crosswind accident.

The airplane's crosswind capability is usually stated in the aircraft manual. If not, you should estimate the maximum acceptable crosswind component equal to one-third of your plane's stall speed.

Setting Minimums

Once you have considered the hazards within the various elements of aviation weather, establish your own personal preflight weather minimums. Be sure your personal minimums allow for some further deterioration in weather to occur after you have left the vicinity of your departure airport. If, for example, you decide you don't want to navigate cross-country beneath a cloud deck of less than 4,000 feet, you might decide you won't take off unless you have a ceiling of at least 4,500 feet. Then if en route clouds start to lower, you have time to head for your alternate en route airport.

Similarly, if you decide that six miles visibility is your minimum for comfortable, safe flight, then you may wish to peg your cross-country departure minimum at seven miles. If you feel moderate turbulence is the maximum bouncing you want for your passengers, then depart only when the forecast calls for no more than light-to-moderate turbulence.

Once you have established your personal weather minimums, reduce them to writing, (see Figure 3-1) and in a form you can carry aboard. A back logbook page is convenient. The time to establish your personal minimums is now. Do not put it off until you are faced with an impending flight.

Your *own* guidelines, in writing, will help reinforce preflight decisions concerning marginal weather conditions. Referring to your written guidelines greatly offsets the "let's get going" pressures which often push pilots into conditions logic tells them are beyond the capability of their equipment or their skill.

Personal Weather Minimums

• Minimum Reported Visibility: _____ mi.

• Minimum Reported Cloud Bases: _____ ft.

• Maximum Extent of Precip.:

_____ Widely Scattered (under 25% areal coverage)

_____ Scattered (25-54% areal coverage)

_____ Widespread (over 55% areal coverage)

• Maximum Reported or Forecast Turbulence:

_____ Light (momentary slight changes in altitude and attitude)

_____ Moderate (aircraft remains in positive control)

_____ Severe (aircraft momentarily out of control)

_____ Extreme (aircraft impossible to control; may cause structural damage)

• Maximum Expected Crosswind Component: _____ kts.

Figure 3-1
Reduce your personal weather minimums to writing, and in a form you can carry aboard: a back page of your logbook is convenient.

Chapter 4

Moonlight Missions

Night flight! The words conjure feelings of pioneering, exploration, and adventure. Stars above and ahead seem closer than Earth below, and the pilot's element makes a subtle shift from *airspace* to simply *space*.

Minutes are suspended in the darkened cockpit. Dimly glowing instruments hold time and motion at rest. Earthbound clamor cannot penetrate the sanctuary of silence within the engine's steady rumble. Even fellow pilots aboard seldom disturb the solitude; they, too, respect the moment. Words are as spartan as movements and each is directed toward a purpose. Here, you can chance to think your own thoughts — to consider the reality of *up here* and *down there*. And the shimmering planet held centered in the windscreen seems a more likely destination than the winking beacon ahead and below. It's the stuff night skies are made of.

Personal Decision

Cross-country night flight is a personal decision. There is little doubt night flight presents a greater element of hazard than daytime flying. The same holds true for nighttime driving. The reason for each is simple — we can't see as well at night. And what we *do* see at night is not always what it seems.

Night skies have their illusions; illusions which rank high as contributing factors of night-flying accidents. Our perception of distance and time are a good example. At night, without abundant landmarks, distance appears compressed. What appears to be five miles is actually ten; what seems 100 AGL is really 200. And since our perception of time draws in part from the passing landmarks, minutes seem to drag. What feels like three minutes might be only one. Your clock will give the facts.

Points of light often misinform. Picture departing over dark, void terrain with a light in the distance ahead. Should you inadvertently elevate the nose, that new view of the light makes it appear you are much higher than you really are. Without reference to the altimeter, you could be fooled into an early level off; not good if sloping terrain lies ahead. A line of distant lights at an angle to your flight path sure looks like a slanting horizon and can trick you into thinking one wing is low and the nose high. Only the attitude indicator can tell you for certain. A point of light abeam an airplane climbing out has its own fib to tell. If the plane's wings are banked toward the point when you spot the light, it looks like the plane is low — that you are not climbing. Confirmation from the VSI reveals the truth.

Even rain on the windscreen lets those ground lights deceive us. Refraction through water on the windscreen bends the light much as it "bends" the soda straw in a glass of coke. It makes us look higher than the altimeter says. Ground lights can even confuse our sense of direction when flying at night. During daylight, we subconsciously use known landmarks or uniform section lines to help guide us. But at night, irregular light patterns can confuse us. We need to rely on our heading indicator for guidance.

If all this sounds like night flight requires better than average instrument interpretive skill, it's true. A few sessions with an instrument instructor will not qualify a VFR pilot for weather flying, but good instrument interpretation will help dispel the illusions of night skies. And time spent with an instrument instructor through skies that meet the criteria of your own personal night-weather minimums will add safety and confidence to your VFR night flying.

Night-Flying Weather Minimums

Pilots setting up their own night-flying weather minimums would do well to review factors which seem to repeat themselves in night accident after night accident. Heavy weather isn't normally in nighttime accident reports. Most pilots know better than to set out in the dark with steady rain, low ceilings, or poor visibility. Typically, the pilot of an ill-fated night flight is non-instrument rated. In examining reports, one finds the flight was often conducted in reasonable visibility, but with light showers in the vicinity. One often finds, too, that the flight went down in a brief shower over an unpopulated area. The pilot had good visibility, only scattered showers and an unpopulated terrain. However, the pilot could not see the rain showers or clouds in time to avoid them, particularly over unlit countryside.

Light rain pilots can easily see through in daylight reduces nighttime forward visibility with an instant smear of IFR across the windscreen. With no lights below for even the most meager sort of reference, the light turbulence of rain, plus a dash of vertigo, and loss of aircraft control is very possible.

The VFR pilot, then, should modify any daylight weather minimums for night flight. You may well want to double the standards for visibility, and cloud coverage and height.

Visibility

At night, visibility distance is harder to establish from the cockpit, and deteriorating visibility is often difficult to discern. I have a pilot friend with several hundred flight hours who thoroughly enjoys night flying. She has some good words concerning visibility and VFR night flying.

"Prevailing visibility is a major concern to me when planning a night flight. I want at least 12 miles, coupled with a favorable forecast for the evening. This may seem too conservative to many, but I don't think so — I've done a *lot* of night flying. The 12 miles of visibility reassures me that, should visibility drop another mile or two, I'm still OK.

"My plane is single-engine. I maintain that engine carefully, but I know it can quit. The prospect of a day-time off-airport landing doesn't frighten me; I can handle that. But the prospect of an off-airport landing at night is another matter. At night, I want a runway within easy reach; one I can find. Therefore, I want to see far enough that I have an airport beacon in sight 90% of the time. I want visibility that has the next beacon nearly in sight as the one behind fades from view. I often need to plan a crooked route to make this possible, but the extra time en route is worth the insurance. Unbeaconed airports just won't do — just try to locate that airport when your need to get it on the ground is critical.

"Then there's the matter of spotting traffic in a timely manner. Navigation lights aren't the easiest things to find, particularly at relatively low altitude around city lights. Then, once you spot them, it takes several glances to determine their altitude, range and heading. Let's say I'm flying at night through only eight miles visibility. If that traffic's speed is just 50% greater than my own plane, I'll close the eight miles in one minute and 36 seconds. In that time, I'd need to first spot the traffic, determine its altitude, distance and track, then decide if it presented a hazard, then decide what I need to do, then move the controls, then let the plane respond to the controls... and still leave enough time for my plane to move out of the way. There's just too many "thens;" it could take one minute and 36 seconds for all of that to happen.

"Then I must consider that even in my short flying career, I've encountered three planes running at night without lights. Did a pilot inadvertently switch them off, did a fuse blow, or did the pilot just forget? Who knows? Fortunately, in each case the night was CAVU and their shapes were seen in the starlight as ghostly images. Would I have seen them through restricted visibility? Maybe.

"I enjoy night flight. It's the only time my schedule lets me fly. But I *do* want at least 12 miles visibility before I take off."

Cloud Coverage

Cloud coverage gains new emphasis at night. A 6,000-foot broken or overcast ceiling during the day presents little difficulty to VFR flying. At night, however, cloud cover hides too many of the stars which help us over dark areas. Or a sloping overcast seen above reflected city lights is particularly deceitful. With the horizon hidden in darkness, the pilot often tries to hold wings parallel to the cloud base. This can quickly produce vertigo.

Low scattered clouds present three major hazards to night VFR. First, you can fly right into them without much warning — and someone else may be doing the same from the other side. Second, if you decide to stay beneath cloud level, other pilots may have, too. You force yourself to fly in a narrow band of congested airspace. Third, if you decide to fly "on top," you run a high risk of getting caught on top, a very uncomfortable nighttime VFR situation. With the cooling temperatures of night, a scattered layer can quickly close to broken or overcast and you often cannot see it happening.

Pilots planning a night cross-country should modify their daytime VFR personal weather minimums (See Figure 4-1). It isn't unreasonable for a pilot to decide against night flying when even scattered precip, light-to-moderate turbulence, or brisk wind is forecast.

Crosswind landing capability can diminish at night. A pilot depends on quick visual references during the round-out to detect drift and alignment. In daylight, these visual clues are all around.

Personal Weather Minimums for Night Operations

• Reported and Forecast Visibility: _____ mi.

• Reported and Forecast Cloud Cover:

_____ Scattered (less than 50% cover)

_____ Broken (more than 50% cover)

_____ Overcast (entire coverage)

• Minimum Acceptable Cloud Bases: _____ft.

• VFR "on top" Operations: _____ yes; _____ no

• Maximum Extent of Reported or Forecast Precip:

_____ None

_____ Widely Scattered (under 25% areal coverage)

_____ Scattered (25-54% areal coverage)

• Maximum Reported or Forecast Turbulence:

_____ None

_____ Light (momentary slight changes in altitude and attitude)

_____ Moderate (larger changes in altitude and attitude but positive aircraft control remains)

• Maximum expected crosswind component: _____kts.

• Recent "hooded" practice: within _____ months

Figure 4-1
Pilots planning a night cross-country should modify their daytime VFR personal weather minimums. Recent hood practice is strongly recommended, as well.

At night, visual references are confined to that egg-shaped patch of a plane's landing light.

A pilot's decision to fly at night and personal weather criteria are individual matters. All depends on the degree of skill and experience the pilot brings to the cockpit. To those pilots inexperienced in night flying but contemplating nighttime cross-country trips: get several hours of dual cross-country planning and training over both familiar and unfamiliar territory at night. Be familiar with the potential for problems, then evaluate your experience and comfort level and decide on your own night-flying weather minimums.

Chapter 5

Accident Potential Assessment

Pilot error doesn't just happen, it's deliberately created. In one instance, a pilot arriving on downwind radioed the tower that he'd just run out of gas. He safely made his emergency landing and our tug went to tow him in. I recognized the shaken pilot as he climbed from the cockpit behind his wife and young son — he'd overflown an airport just 30 miles northwest, and the fuel gauges had to have been bouncing on empty even then. When he had a few moments, I walked over and asked, "Why?" He answered quite honestly, "Because my wife's folks were waiting for us, and I didn't want to worry them."

Every year, good, logical-thinking pilots come to grief because they suddenly act in an illogical, inexplicable manner. As we hear the account or read the report, it's easy to think we'd never do such a thing. But, in truth, we all hold within us a real potential for tragedy — a time bomb.

Put simply, it's a matter of misplaced priority. It's so absolutely easy for any one of us to momentarily forget piloting's number-one goal: the safety of both plane and passengers. In almost every instance of pilot error I've seen, the pilot has temporarily displaced this top priority with an earth-bound consideration of lesser value. The moment this happens, that pilot is reaching for an accident and the time bomb starts ticking.

The unreasonable actions of pilots seem to stem from six basic human frailties. Let's look at some examples and watch the priorities bounce.

Vanity, Pride or Illogical Considerations

Two pilots ferried their planes from Texas in close formation. Each was well experienced and thoroughly familiar with the high-performance machine he flew. Midafternoon found them climbing eastward on Victor 20 to stay above the cumulus gathering around them; their tanks were big and they could file IFR if need be.

The Texas border passed down through Sabin Lake and drifted behind them, unseen beneath the broken cloud deck. It was good VFR above the clouds, though maybe a little choppy. Yet that small amount of turbulence only let the two pilots better feel the 200 knots they were clicking off. The clouds pushed higher and, on 122.75, the men talked over whether to stick together flying VFR or file and go their separate IFR ways. They decided to continue VFR.

Towering cumulus punched up through the overcast, bringing rain to the hamlets below. The thunderheads were far enough apart, with clear, cool air between them. Shallow turns detoured the pilots neatly along the airway, and they thought it a good flight.

Two miles above the Louisiana lowlands, something happened that's difficult to explain. While looking at each other through their Plexiglas canopies (I'm sure) and with mic buttons unpressed, the two experienced pilots proceeded to deliberately fly, wingtip to wingtip, into a mature thunderstorm. Once inside the dark, nine-mile-high tempest, there was little they could do to hold back the inevitable. Wind shear and hail pulled the bucking planes apart even as the pilots asked themselves, "Why did we do it?"

Many months later, an airline captain and his copilot taxied their jet onto the runway, surrounded by swirling snow and bitter cold. As they straddled the centerline, they calmly discussed their iced-up wings and then launched into the wet, sticky, frozen sky they knew wouldn't admit them. And in those sinking seconds before impact, even as they quickly acted to avert what they knew was about to happen, I'm certain each asked himself "Why did we?"

The only answer I can come up with is that these pilot errors occurred due to vanity, pride or illogical considerations. I put all three in the same category because they seem to interrelate — I really can't tell where one mental attitude ends and the next begins. I've seen the clues, through. This phenomenon most commonly happens when two pilots are in the same cockpit and the opportunity for a really bad pilot error comes before them. Then both refuse to verbally question what they suppose the other has decided, or perhaps hesitate to be the first to back away from that supposed decision. But even one pilot in the cockpit can do the job quite nicely.

We're all susceptible to vanity and pride; these are human traits. Used properly they add to our enjoyment of life but, used improperly in the cockpit, they become an in-flight hazard. The best alternatives I can suggest is to first ask yourself a question, "Will this action I'm proposing add to the safety of the flight, or am I only acting out of regard for someone's personal feelings?" Second, as a passenger/pilot sensing a pilot error, exert the will to voice your opinion.

Physical Condition and Mental Outlook

All of us have those days when we just can't get things right. If you have trouble simply parking your car in the FBO lot, for goodness sake, don't go flying that day. Similarly, don't climb into the plane when you feel like you're coming down with something. Many pilots do so with the idea that their health will improve with altitude. But it won't; in fact, it will probably get worse. Imagine experiencing the initial distress of the flu when your destination still lies 20 minutes ahead.

We live in a pressure-cooker world. For most people, a certain degree of stress is a normal part of life and doesn't deter us from our daily rounds. But stress can come in hard-to-swallow doses, and each of us has a capacity limit. A few tensed-up pilots even try to use the airplane as a tranquilizer, which is pretty dangerous medicine.

Take a preflight peek into your stress bucket to see if it's nearing the brim. Look for physical signs — tense muscles, stomachache, shaking hands or headache — only you know your own symptoms. If you're nearing your capacity, don't go flying. Chances are, an in-flight stressful situation could run your bucket over, with chances then for a colossal pilot error.

In addition, look toward your mental state that day. A flaring temper can easily push a pilot beyond safety, just to "show 'em who's in charge, anyway." Further, temporary depression or anxiety is another especially grim ghost to turn loose in the cockpit. Either can create a "What's the use?" outlook. If a critical situation calls for instantaneous action, such a state of mind could delay the pilot's response to the point of low-grade suicide.

Alcohol consumption continues to be a high-percentage cause of lightplane accidents resulting in fatalities and, in recent years, this number has risen alarmingly. Regulations demand a minimum of eight hours between the bottle and the throttle (along with a legal maximum of 0.04 percent alcohol in the blood). But is this recovery time enough? In many cases, probably not. If alcohol is a part of your life, consider these facts when it's time to evaluate your flying fitness:

- The average individual reaches the 0.04 blood-alcohol content figure with two drinks in an hour's time.
- It takes the average individual two hours "recovery" time per ounce of alcohol consumed.

- This recovery time is predicated on oxygen available at sea level. At 5,000 feet, the recovery time doubles. (In other words, a pilot could recover at sea level, climb to cruising altitude and experience a partial return of symptoms.)

Fatigue and hunger are often under-rated causes of pilot error. We don't make sound business or personal decisions when we're overtired, so why should our in-flight judgments be any different? Fatigue-induced pilot error often occurs as the destination draws close with its special demands of approach and landing procedures. Make sure your preflight planning accommodates your own personal endurance with rest stops.

Hunger affects different people in different degrees. Some folks can go two days on a celery stalk while others can't function properly without a steak-and-eggs breakfast behind them. Plan your flight to include chow stops or a brown bag to satisfy your needs.

In a Hurry

Boy, don't we make mistakes when we rush? And those errors aren't just confined to hurrying madly through a job. Often, rushed activity can set up mistakes that keep on occurring well after things have seemingly settled down.

Hurried preflight planning often sets up pilot errors that don't manifest themselves until later in the flight. The point here is to allow ample time for planning. It isn't unreasonable for a trip of a few hundred miles to require an hour's worth of planning and preflight activities: checking weather, gauging aircraft performance, calculating weight and balance, laying out the route, researching the destination airport, selecting alternates, looking up frequencies. It all takes time.

Each year, the FAA lists, by frequency of occurrence, the 10 most common causes for pilot error and accidents. For as many years as I can remember, the first-listed cause remains "inadequate preflight preparation and/or planning." If a flight's immediacy won't allow time to safely plan, exert the willpower to postpone the trip — it's just another case of priority.

Defiance of Government Regulations

Let's face it — many individuals today harbor an antagonism toward governmental agencies and bureaus. In recent years, we've felt the weight of heartless, greedy and illogical bureaucratic action that seems to destroy our efforts to simply enjoy a live-and-let-live existence. This is bound to cause a feeling of resentment toward anything governmental or bureaucratic. Yet, in the interest of air safety and the continued efficiency of aviation, we can't look with contempt on the procedures and regulations governing our lives aloft.

Hostility against regulations in the air is often a prelude to senseless disaster. It's a mood that causes a pilot to view a weather briefing with scorn, or delay an ATC demand for immediate action. If you suspect that you're carrying a grudge against the system into the cockpit, remind yourself of four facts:

1. Antagonism often leads to senseless accidents.
2. The folks with whom you think you'd like to get even are in a steel and concrete building on the ground.
3. You're the one hanging in the sky in a flimsy plane.
4. Anger is one letter shy of danger.

Defiance of the system can come from another quarter: the old pro who believes that personal skill and experience elevates a pilot above the rules. Unfortunately, that belief doesn't help this pilot fit in too well with the rest of us, and we must classify that pilot as an in-flight hazard.

"It Won't Happen To Me" Syndrome

An airplane is designed to operate within a very narrow performance range. Weight, stress, aerodynamic ability and aircraft performance are all unyielding values that make no allowances for the wishes of pilots. There's no such thing as a "forgiving airplane." In light aircraft especially, the parameters of these limitations are quite small. Load a lightplane a fraction out of balance, slightly exceed the design load factors, fly the wing a half-degree past its critical angle, or ask it to stay airborne one minute beyond its endurance, and the flight will likely fail.

Similarly, pilots often reach for error when they choose to take on a critical flight situation which demands skill beyond their demonstrated ability. This doesn't mean pilots shouldn't expand their skills, they should — but in a controlled situation. A pilot with mediocre short-field ability, for example, can spend many worthwhile hours sharpening those takeoff and landing skills on the middle 2,000 feet of a long runway. But that same pilot would be ill-advised to take existing mediocre skill into a real 2,000-foot strip.

There's a popular feeling among pilots that when faced with a truly critical situation, we'll react beyond our normal ability. This is rarely true. It has been my observation that when we're really behind the eight ball, we often react with far less than our usual skill and judgment.

Get-Home-Itis

Without doubt, for some pilots the homeward flight is often a "go at any cost" affair. I've noticed this common thread running through many instances of poor judgment. The pilot may feel pressed to go because someone has arranged to meet the flight at the destination airport. If you find yourself subscribing to get-home-itis for this reason in particular, consider this: don't arrange

Personal Preflight Questionnaire

♦ Is every decision based on fact and free of vanity?

♦ Is your physical condition at its best and free of any symptoms that signal possible impairment at altitude?

♦ Has an adequate time elapsed since the consumption of any alcohol in order to prevent a reoccurrence of symptoms at altitude?

♦ Are you beginning the flight free of fatigue?

♦ Are you beginning the flight with your personal stress load well below its maximum capacity?

♦ Have you allowed adequate time for an unhurried preflight preparation?

♦ Is every preflight decision in accordance with established procedure and regulation?

♦ Are the anticipated demands of the flight within your demonstrated capability?

♦ Is the flight totally free of the "I'm going, regardless" syndrome?

Figure 5-1
Unless each question can be answered with an honest and unqualified "yes," the flight has a high accident potential.

to have someone waiting for your arrival. Call them after you and your passengers are safely on the ground.

Human weakness often leads good pilots into illogical actions and pilot error. Who needs bad weather or a malfunctioning airplane for enemies when these six human problems lie within? While the frailties may seem a bit nebulous, the results are frequently only too real. And every one of us is susceptible. As a final preflight defense, let me make a last suggestion: anytime you feel outside pressures pushing you into an action that defies your logic, leave the airport (see Figure 5-1). You'll be surprised how quickly the pressure dissolves when the waiting airplane is no longer in sight.

Part II

Departure

I have lifted my plane from the Nairobi airport for perhaps a thousand flights and I have never felt her wheels glide from the earth into the air without knowing the uncertainty and the exhilaration of firstborn adventure.

Beryl Markham, *West with the Night*

Chapter 6

Evaluating Real-Life Takeoff Performance

You would never expect to see an experienced pilot contemplating a departure, step to the nose of the plane, and say, "Listen airplane, in a few minutes I'm going to lift off from this runway. Now remember, I've faithfully changed your oil every 25 hours and done everything else right by you... besides, there are some deserving people depending on this flight. So, when I mash on your throttle, I want you to give beyond yourself. OK?"

Experienced pilots know they cannot depend on chance or special favor from their plane. They know they cannot expect the plane to make allowances and perform beyond its capability, such as climbing safely away from a strip too short for the temperature, running through a crosswind which exceeds a design limitation, or delivering an uneventful departure when loaded aft of limits. Aware pilots know their actions are subject to the basic truth of flying, which simply says: plane and sky accept no excuses and grant no special considerations. It makes no difference whether we walk earth, as good or bad, wise or foolish, poor or rich. When we enter the cockpit, we leave behind our earthbound differences. We touch the controls as one — a pilot. If our actions are *right*, the flight will probably succeed. If our actions are *not* right, the flight may likely fail.

Your takeoff planning must totally reckon the task asked of the plane against the facts and figures of the manufacturer's performance charts and tables. Yet you must remember the manufacturer's idealistic performance figures are only approximate when set to real-life situations. The variables affecting takeoff are often difficult to accurately standardize and evaluate; the softness of runway surface, or the headwind component of a runway breeze are two such examples. The most nebulous of all is pilot technique.

Takeoff Performance Variables

There are 11 variables that affect takeoff performance on every departure:

1. Flap position
2. Airspeed
3. Runway surface
4. Aircraft weight
5. Headwind
6. Crosswind component
7. Field elevation
8. Runway temperature
9. Obstacle clearance
10. Abort/stop distance
11. Pilot technique

Only by understanding how each variable affects performance can the pilot totally and professionally preplan by relating the performance tables to real-life conditions.

Flap Position

Most aircraft manuals clearly state the recommended flap setting for a normal takeoff. It may take careful reading, however, to find the recommended flap position with which to clear obstacles. But find it you must if there are obstacles to clear, because the flap setting that facilitates a shorter ground run often decreases maximum climb performance. The manufacturer has spent untold hours of practical demonstration in order to determine what works best for their airplane. Study and adhere to your plane's flight manual recommendations for the takeoff situation at hand.

Airspeed

Your aircraft manual specifies three airspeeds relating to takeoffs. **Rotate speed** is that point at which you apply additional back pressure to gain lift off. Don't guess at this critical airspeed; consult your flight manual. If you use an incorrect liftoff speed, you lengthen takeoff distance. Leave it on the ground too long, you suffer frictional drag; break away too soon, you suffer aerodynamic drag.

The **best-angle of climb speed** is the precise speed that delivers the most altitude for the *horizontal distance* flown. It is the speed you hit when obstacles reach into your departure path. Any other speed costs you safety when clearing an obstacle. This airspeed is often stated as "IAS at 50 feet" on the takeoff chart.

By **best-rate of climb speed**, the aircraft manual means that airspeed which, with the recommended climb power applied, gains the greatest altitude in the least *time* flown, consistent with engine cooling. It is the speed you set your plane at after clearing any obstacle. This airspeed is often stated in the plane's rate of climb chart. It is important you do indeed climb at the recommended power and speed. Any speed above or below not only costs climb efficiency, but also causes undue engine wear.

Runway Surface

Many takeoff charts contemplate only a dry paved runway that provides good acceleration to liftoff speed. But the times you are most concerned with takeoff distance usually occur when you face a grass-strip departure. If your manual does not provide grass-strip figures, use a rule of thumb: add 20% for dry grass; 50% if the grass needs mowing or is wet.

Another real-life runway condition seldom charted is runway slope. It's a difficult factor to pin down, particularly on a "one-way" strip that may call for a tailwind departure. Here, I might add, a one-way takeoff is almost never a matter of the runway's slope; it's usually higher terrain upslope from the runway that stops the action. Your best preflight evaluation is a discussion with the airport operator; that operator best knows how your plane will perform on that runway.

Proper tire inflation goes hand in hand with runway surface and performance chart predictions. Under-inflation can easily increase takeoff distance by 15% or more. Consult your flight manual for the recommended air pressure; the same tire, mounted on different light planes, will carry different inflations, ranging from 20 psi to 40 psi for proper takeoff performance.

Aircraft Weight

Remember the big surprise you got on your first solo takeoff? For many it was the alarmingly quick liftoff without the instructor's ballast aboard. The lighter the load your plane carries, the less time and distance it requires to accelerate to flying speed. Some aircraft manuals provide only maximum allowable gross weight performance figures. In this case apply a rule of thumb: for lightly loaded takeoffs, you may reduce the charted distance by 5% for each 100 pounds below maximum allowable weight. This explains why experienced pilots are sometimes seen defueling to half tanks and ferrying passengers out one by one to a nearby larger airport when the takeoff from a short field is tight.

Headwind

An oncoming wind reduces the time and distance it takes your plane to accelerate to flying speed, simply because the wind flow already has the wing "moving" through the air before the plane starts rolling. Estimate your headwind component from the wind sock by applying some rules of thumb: 15 knots stiffens a sock; seven to eight knots has it drooping at a 45° angle. If the sock shows the breeze within 30° of runway alignment, estimate three-fourth the full velocity as your headwind component (see Figure 6-1). If the wind lies between 30 and 60°, plan on half the velocity as a headwind. A wind that blows across the runway at 60° or more, with normal velocity, has little headwind effect. If your aircraft manual does not provide for various headwind components, as a rule of thumb, reduce the zero-wind distance by 15% for each ten knots of headwind component.

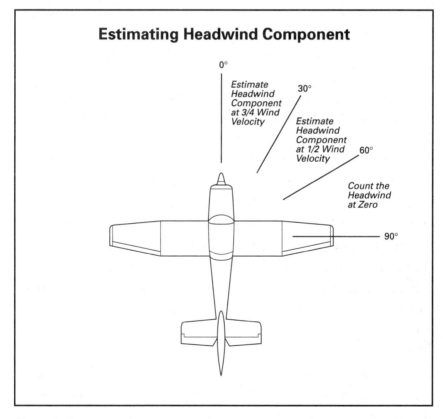

Figure 6-1
These conservative estimates reflect the fact that wind rarely blows constant in direction or velocity.

Crosswind Component

Each make and model has a maximum crosswind component it can safely accept. There is a limit beyond which there is just not enough control deflection available. This critical crosswind component is often stated in the plane's manual, but if not, apply a rule of thumb: do not attempt a takeoff when the component exceeds 25% of the plane's stall speed. To estimate the crosswind component, use other rules of thumb (See Figure 6-2):

1. If the sock shows the wind within 30° of runway alignment, estimate the crosswind component at one-half the wind's velocity.
2. If the wind lies from 30 to 60° across the runway, estimate the crosswind component at three-fourths the wind's velocity.
3. If the wind blows from 60 to 90° across the runway, estimate the component to equal the velocity. These conservative estimates reflect the fact that wind rarely blows at a constant velocity and direction.

Field Elevation

The higher you are, the farther apart the molecules (lower atmospheric pressure allows them to spread apart) and the thinner the air. The wings must move faster to have the same mass of air molecules flowing over them. At higher elevation, then, you will need greater distance for acceleration to the faster true flying speed. And, at the same time, the engine only has thin air to breathe. This means less fuel to burn for power if you properly lean for elevation; if you do not lean an over-rich mixture occurs. Either way, thin air reduces engine output; acceleration and climb suffer.

If your manual does not chart performance at various field elevations, use a rule of thumb: light aircraft generally require an extra 25% of runway for each 1,000 feet above sea level.

Runway Temperature

Heat produces the same detriment to takeoff performance as a high field elevation — spread-out molecules give thin air. Wings and engine just do not get the chance to do their very best. In the absence of manual figures for temperature, apply a rule of thumb: add 10% to the chart's distance for each 25°F above the standard temperature for that elevation. (Estimate sea-level "standard temperature" at 60°F; subtract 10° per 2,500 feet for standard at field elevation. Estimate runway temperature with your OAT gauge.)

The greatest temperature problem arises when you combine a hot afternoon with a high elevation airport. Most pilots are amazed

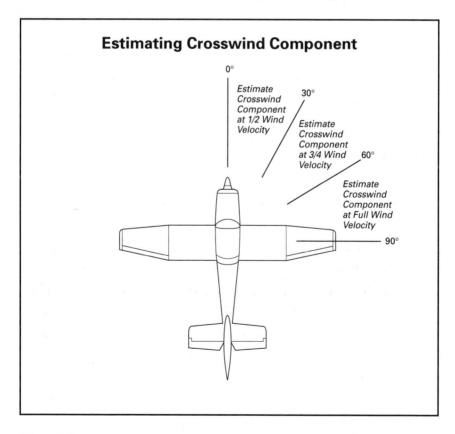

Figure 6-2
These conservative estimates reflect the limitations of a plane's control deflections.

at the decrease in performance the first time they launch from a high, hot runway. Consider any runway less than 3,000 feet a short runway if the elevation exceeds 2,500 feet and the temperature is greater than 80°F. If you have not yet had the experience, make a hot, heavy-load departure from your home airport with the throttle set 200 RPM below your normal takeoff reading. Imagine a 400-foot ridge 3 miles ahead; one you want to clear by 1,000 feet, minimum. This gives a good simulation of the takeoff and climb performance you can expect at a field 2,000 feet higher, and an appreciation for reduced rate of climb. Just remember to keep a hand on the throttle in case the action turns too realistic.

Obstacle Clearance

Even if you face no obstacles, it is the longer distance-to-clear-50-foot-obstacle figure that governs your planning. After all, you want to be at least that high as you cross the airport boundary. If you do face an obstacle, remember when using your performance chart that real obstacles off the end of a real runway do not come in standard FAA 50-foot heights. If you estimate the actual obstacle at twice, thrice, or quadruple the 50-foot performance-table height, increase your clearance distance accordingly. To do this, use a rule of thumb: take the difference between "ground run" and "obstacle distance" and apply it to each additional 50 feet of obstacle height.

Most light, single-engine manuals employ the plane's best-angle climb speed over the obstacle. Some, however, recommend a higher speed, even at the cost of climb performance. These manuals state it this way because that plane's best-angle of climb speed is close to, or below, the plane's power-off stall speed. A power failure following takeoff at best-angle could be disastrous. The secret here — know your aircraft manual.

Abort/Stop Distance

Before you begin your takeoff from any runway, determine your stop distance and select a landmark with which to identify its length. If your plane is not off by that point, you can abort the takeoff with little risk of damage. Run beyond that point, however, and you are committed. The plane must lift off or suffer damage.

Very few light single-engine manuals state an abort/stop distance. I suggest a rule of thumb: use the landing roll distance required for the conditions (plus 50% margin for error) for your abort/stop distance, since liftoff and touchdown speeds are nearly the same.

Pilot Technique

Pilot technique addresses the skill, knowledge, and judgement that you bring to the cockpit. If you asked me to state four paramount rules with which to implement pilot technique, I'd list:

1. Relate each takeoff situation to the plane's performance charts. It is so easy, as we prepare for takeoff, to say to ourselves: "That is an approved runway before me; I am flying an approved airplane; therefore, everything will work out OK." To say this, is to say we are willing to rely on past successes. Every takeoff, however, must stand on its own. Even that runway which has accepted your plane so many times in the past may refuse to do so today. For you are now attempting to takeoff with today's load, today's density altitude, today's unique set of takeoff variables.

2. Adhere to the manufacturer's takeoff recommendations. The manufacturer knows what works best for its airplane. There's a bromide directed toward many aircraft which says, "this is a forgiving airplane." But in reality this is true of no airplane. All planes have operating limits. In light planes, especially, the

parameters of these limits are quite narrow in terms of airspeed, loading, power, and aerodynamic forces. Operate the plane within these limits and it will perform as expected. Operate *beyond* these limits, however, and you are breaking new ground. Manufacturers state their tried and proven procedures with the express motive of keeping pilots within the design limits of operation.

3. Plan an abort point before the takeoff gets underway. Don't leave this important decision until the moment to employ it is at hand. If you do not already hold the commitment to abort if necessary, you may be subconsciously committed to "press on regardless" when things start going wrong.

    I'm convinced that had pilots executed a timely abort, 90% of the takeoff accidents would never have happened. Accordingly, I advise my students: when planning a takeoff, hold in mind your primary plan to abort. Then, if everything is still OK before you reach your abort point, put your *secondary* plan into action — complete the takeoff.

4. Plan an adequate safety margin of runway length. The unforeseen can creep into any takeoff — a headwind that decides to die, a cockpit distraction that costs aircraft control and runway length, a simple misreading of performance charts. As a rule of thumb, I like a runway that exceeds 150% of the calculated minimum distance required.

The takeoff is normally the most critical phase of flight; close to the ground, low airspeed, minimum maneuvering room, dependent upon maximum performance from both plane and pilot. Launching an aircraft is no trivial matter and cannot be handled in a cavalier manner; a pilot cannot just "pour on the coal" and hope to get away from the ground before anything bad happens. Safety

Evaluating Takeoff Performance

Recommended flap setting: _____ deg.

Recommended rotate speed: _____ kts.

Recommended best angle speed: _____ kts.

Power-off stall speed (30 deg. bank): _____ kts.

Runway surface: _____ paved; _____ unpaved; _____ soft

Proper tire inflation: _____ psi

Gross weight (balance verified): _____ lbs.

Aircraft allowable gross weight: _____ lbs.

Headwind component: _____ kts.

Crosswind component: _____ kts.

Aircraft maximum allowable crosswind: _____ kts.

Field elevation: _____ MSL

Runway temperature: OAT _____ deg.

Distance needed for each additional 50 feet of obstacle height: _____ ft.

Abort / stop distance required: _____ ft.

Calculated runway length required: _____ ft.

Extra length for safety margin: _____ ft.

Total takeoff distance desired: _____ ft.

Rate of climb at field elevation and temperature: _____ ft./min.

Rate of climb required to clear obstacles or terrain ahead by a safe margin: _____ ft./min.

Figure 6-3
Relate the accumulated facts to performance charts, actual environment and pilot skill.

demands that we research the 11 variables which affect takeoff performance and relate them to the actual environment, the aircraft's capability within that environment, and the pilot's skill (See Figure 6-3). To do otherwise is to rely upon chance. And the very nature of chance is that it must someday turn against us.

Chapter 7

Takeoff Balancing Act

Several summers ago over south Florida, ATC received a call from a training flight. The instructor advised that he and the student (a commercial pilot going for her CFI) were going to commence a practice spin. They were to start from 4,500 feet and planned to recover by 3,000. The plane was a popular four-place trainer-type. A few moments after the initial call, ATC received this one: "Mayday! Mayday! It won't come out!" And it didn't.

Months later, a similar accident happened in a similar low-performance trainer. Here, an extremely experienced instructor had conducted stall recovery with a primary student. The plane stalled, spun, and never recovered. The investigations of both accidents turned up some facts which make a pilot stop and think.

First, each cockpit had an experienced pilot at the controls. Second, each aircraft was a type we often call "forgiving." Third, depending on the weight and balance, each plane could either be a *normal* or *utility* category aircraft, with spins approved only if loaded in the utility balance range. Fourth, while each aircraft was loaded within the normal category limits, it had exceeded the aft limits for utility. And finally, each plane exceeded these aft limits by less than a half-inch.

Interesting, isn't it, just how critical weight and balance can be in light aircraft. And yet departing pilots are seldom seen with their noses buried in the weight and balance charts doing their pre-takeoff calculations as the suitcases and passengers climb aboard.

Of course, grief does not come to all planes loaded slightly out of balance. Many of those flights succeed. It usually takes the onset of a stall to trigger the disaster, such as one produced by a cockpit distraction on initial climbout, the combination of slow speed and load factors when S-turning on final for spacing, or a pitch attitude that goes unnoticed during a go-around. To guard against the disastrous combination of improper balance and the inadvertent stall, learn how to use your plane's weight and balance data. Some manual presentations are simple to use. Others are not. If you are unsure about the graph and table procedures, have an instructor guide you through some sample loadings (See Figure 7-1).

When should a pilot calculate weight and balance? As a general rule of thumb, during the preflight checkup, run a weight and balance calculation anytime the seating capacity is over half filled, when there is luggage in any baggage compartment, or if extreme aft seating is employed.

And of course, run a careful calculation before any training flight that involves stalls, no matter how "forgiving" the plane, or how the weight is distributed. As an example, the plane I fly day in and day out is a garden-variety two-seat trainer — about as docile as they come. Yet with a student aboard that slightly bests my own weight, and the seat shoved back to accommodate my big feet, the plane is unsafe to stall. With the tanks topped off it is a tad over allowable gross and just barely aft of limits — a little less than half an inch, as a matter of fact. (How do I solve this problem? I train these students in my plane's bigger sibling.)

For the sake of our passengers, ourselves, and our plane, pilots cannot afford to guess at weight and balance. The preflight research necessary to evaluate the plane's capability against the task we set before it does take time and effort, certainly. But to fly with safety, there is no other way.

Sample Loading Situations

Baggage * Passenger * Fuel

A. Baggage Weight Allowable With:

    1. All seats occupied/full tanks: _____ lbs.

    2. Front seats occupied/full tanks: _____ lbs.

    3. All seats occupied/partial (____ gal.) tanks: _____ lbs.

    4. Front seats occupied/partial (____ gal.) tanks: _____ lbs.

B. Rear-Seat Weight Allowable with Front Seats Occupied And:

    1. Baggage to capacity/full tanks: _____ lbs.

    2. Baggage to capacity/partial (____ gal.) tanks: _____ lbs.

    3. No baggage/full tanks: _____ lbs.

    4. No baggage/partial (____ gal.) tanks: _____ lbs.

C. Fuel Weight Allowable With:

    1. All seats occupied/baggage to capacity: _____ lbs.

    2. All seats occupied/no baggage: _____ lbs.

    3. Front seats occupied/baggage to capacity: _____ lbs.

    4. Front seats occupied/no baggage: _____ lbs.

Figure 7-1
If you are unsure about how to use your plane's weight and balance data, have an instructor guide you through some sample loadings.

Chapter 8

Stall Attitudes: Mental and Angular

The stall/spin accident continues to produce a major portion of our light plane fatalities. For as many years as I can remember these accidents have occurred at a one-per-day rate. Many of these stalls (which offered easy recovery) turned into accidents simply because the pilots involved let their "stall anxiety" inhibit prompt recovery action.

Many pilots harbor an illogical anxiety toward the stall attitude. If this common concern is true in your case, you are not alone. Let me recount an incident that occurred several years ago — it might put your concerns to rest.

Attitudes of Mind and Pitch

The summer morning breeze puffing through the open hangar brought a whiff of creosote from the heating tarmac ramp. It was still cool in the shaded corner where I sat at my oil-stained wooden desk, but I knew the afternoon students were in for some uncomfortable hours.

Several uncowled airplanes, including a perfectly restored little tailwheel J-3, were parked in different stages of tear-down, and the pleasant ring of a dropped wrench drifted across the hangar. Outside, a mechanic was running up the engine in one of my three trainers. (It was the 4-year old ship, which we referred to as "the new plane.")

The other two planes were out on solo cross-countries, and I'd spent most of the morning trying to figure out how to squeeze an unpalatable fuel increase into a palatable hourly rental increase. I was no closer to a solution when Tom Cutter walked in. He had to wait a moment for the trainer's engine on the other side of the metal hangar wall to rev down before he could speak.

"Ron, you got a minute?" he asked.

"Have a seat," I said, and scooped the pile of old aviation magazines from the folding metal chair, and filed them on top of the even older issues stacked against the wall.

Tom Cutter had earned his pilot certificate three years ago at another airport and now had about 200 hours. He enjoys flying on the weekends and recently bought his first plane — a real nice red and white used Cherokee.

Tom sat down. He leaned back in the chair and reached over to toy with the small brass RON FOWLER - FLYING INSTRUCTOR desktop sign that for years had been my sole advertising program.

He said, "I've been up giving the Cherokee a workout and I think I've got a problem with my flying."

"Oh?" I said to fill the pause.

"I think so," he repeated.

"What happened?"

"Well, I was practicing stalls," he said. "And I'll tell you, doing those things scare me as much now as when I first learned them."

It's a common anxiety, of course, but Tom didn't know that. He only knew that *he* didn't like stalls.

"How can I get over being nervous about them?" he asked. "Or am I just stuck with it forever? I don't even know *why* they worry me."

I thought of one big reason why many pilots often harbor anxiety toward stalls: being forced into stall recovery practice before they've had a chance to learn positive aircraft control in normal attitudes. Most students use their common sense in the cockpit. And, when they're asked to fly the plane through a stall, they *know* they're dealing with a critical attitude. If they aren't satisfied with their *normal* aircraft control, they know that stall recovery practice is asking for something they are ill prepared to deliver. How much better it would be for student and instructor alike, if fledglings didn't discover stalls and stall recoveries until *after* they've mastered straight and level, turns, climbs, descents, ground reference maneuvers and even landings in dual flight. But this was all past history for Tom. He wanted to know how he could cure his anxiety now. And the answer was simple.

I reached up and took the model Skyhawk from the shelf against the hangar wall. Out on the ramp I heard the whispering engine from one of the returning 150s as my student pulled it into its tie-down spot. The student revved the engine slightly for a few seconds, to rid it of 100LL deposits, then shut down with a clack-clack-clack.

"Tom, most pilots who don't like stalls feel that way because they have a misconception of the stall attitude. Many pilots hold an exaggerated opinion of the plane's pitch when the stall occurs."

I handed the model Skyhawk to Tom. "Show me what you think the pitch attitude looks like when the stall breaks."

"About like so," he answered, holding the model's nose pitched up about 50°.

"Nope. You have the nose pitched way too high. And it's your exaggerated idea of the stall attitude that's causing your anxiety."

"Why is that?"

"Because your exaggerated idea of the stall's pitch attitude leads you to a couple of mistaken ideas of what the plane *might* do when the stall breaks," I said.

Tom looked at the model airplane and said, "I'm not sure what I *do* think might happen."

"I believe there are a couple of specters in the back of your mind about what might result from the stall," I said. "Specters brought about by your idea of a too-steep stall attitude."

Tom looked at the model again and tried to picture himself in the cockpit. I went on.

"I think the back of your mind sees your plane either sliding downhill tail first, or flopping over on its back, when the stall breaks — and either vision is enough to make the most stout heart falter."

Tom's head started nodding with understanding and agreement.

"Of course, neither of those things will happen," I said.

"Why not?"

"Because your plane just isn't tilted up that high. Tom, would you believe that your plane's nose is tilted only about 13 or 14° when the stall breaks?" (See Figure 8-1.)

"That's pretty hard to believe," he said. "It sure seems a heck of a lot steeper when I'm doing them."

"That's because of your myopic viewpoint when the plane stalls. Look at it this way, where are your eyes pointed when the stall breaks?"

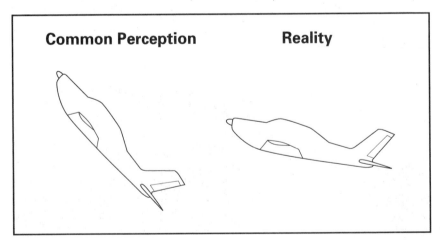

Figure 8-1
Many pilots visualize the stall attitude as a 50 to 60° angle from the plane's path of flight. A 15° angle to the flight path is nearer the truth.

"Right out over the nose."

"Exactly ... and you see only ..."

"Sky," he finished.

"And it *looks* like you're pointed straight up to outer space because you don't see any visual references," I said. "If you want to see your true stall attitude, look out at your wingtip. You'd see the slant of your wingtip relative to the horizon way less than 20°."

"Even power-on stalls?"

"Only about 2° more in most planes," I said. "But in no way steep enough to produce an imagined tail-slide or back-flop."

"What *does* the plane do when it stalls?"

"It settles about 20 feet in the stall attitude — trying to land — then the nose eases downward."

Tom looked at the model plane he had put on the desk. He pushed the tail down slightly with his finger, trying to mentally reduce his 50° pitch attitude concept to the 13 or 14° I'd promised him.

"Tom," I said, standing and pointing to the little J-3 parked in the hangar, "if you want to take an unhurried look at the stall

Figure 8-2
A good look at a parked taildragger reveals the true stall attitude.

attitude, just look at any parked tailwheel airplane. We land 'em in a full stall, and *that's* the true stall attitude (See Figure 8-2).

"I hadn't thought of it that way."

"Well," I said, "when you realize how tame the stall attitude is, you stop worrying about those things that just won't happen."

"I think I'll take the Cherokee up for a few more minutes," he said as we walked toward the open hangar door into the bright mid-morning sunshine.

We said so long and he walked across the ramp toward his plane, slowing a little as he passed to look at a parked, Cessna 180 tailwheeler. I turned back to my beat-up desk, sat down, looked at the fuel bills, glanced up at my rental rates posted on the wall and tried once more to fit the square peg into the round hole.

Guarding Against Low-Altitude Stalls

Pilots often wonder how a stall can accidentally come to the cockpit. After all, your stall practice clearly shows the warnings an on-coming stall gives: the sight of a low airspeed indication or pitched nose, the sound of the stall horn or the fading rush of slipstream across the canopy, the feel of sagging aileron control or the final buffet. How, you might wonder, can an accidental stall slip up on you unnoticed. The answer in a word — distraction.

Nearly every accidental approach to a stall I have witnessed had it's origin in a distraction which momentarily made the pilot forget the number one priority — flying the airplane. Examples are easy to imagine. For instance, a pilot, turning base to final, still searching out closing traffic on a long straight-in. Or a pilot, while executing a go-around in an out-of-trim plane, gets concerned with communicating to the tower. Or even the pilot flying low and slow, then turning too steeply to inspect a point of interest on the ground.

You must try to avoid distractions which might allow you to momentarily forget your number one priority — maintaining aircraft control. Basic aircraft control simply means the pilot is in positive control of the plane's three basic elements: altitude, heading and airspeed. Unless you have these three elements under positive control, you have no business attending to other matters such as communicating with a controller, sorting out navigation, or even attending to an aircraft malfunction. If distraction robs a pilot of basic aircraft control, a stall is a distinct possibility.

Yet, we are only human. And we know that distractions *can* occur, no matter how closely we try to remain vigilant. Therefore, to further guard against an unintentional stall at low altitude (where they hold the greatest hazard) consider putting these ten rules of thumb into play when you fly within 1,500 feet of the ground:

1. Avoid flying at speeds lower than your plane's "flaps-up" approach speed (figure this minimum speed as 1.3 x flaps-up stall speed).
2. Avoid any maneuvering that requires a bank in excess of 30° (to avoid excess aerodynamic loading).
3. Run your engine at a setting no lower than 55% of power (to assure greater airflow across the wing with prop wash).
4. Keep one hand on the throttle so it's already there if you need it (time can be a critical factor in preventing a stall).
5. Fly with one notch of flaps extended (to provide a greater cushion between flying speed and stalling speed).
6. Run the engine with carburetor heat full hot (be sure to lean the fuel mixture to guard against the over-rich condition that carburetor heat produces).
7. Avoid pitch attitudes which cover the horizon with the cowl (if you can't see the horizon you can only guess at the pitch attitude).

8. Don't study a ground object which lies behind your shoulders (if you need a better look, turn the airplane).

9. Make certain the plane is trimmed properly for the airspeed being flown (an out-of-trim plane just begs a pilot to let attentions wander).

10. Cut cockpit chatter to a minimum and, if possible, avoid dealing with an aircraft discrepancy at low altitudes (the plane's attitude, heading and airspeed demand your fullest attentions).

There is one final thing we must keep foremost in our minds when reacting to an inadvertent stall at low altitude. We *must* conform to our trained reflex actions rather than fall victim to our natural instinct (see Figure 8-3). A fully developed stall may point your nose toward the ground. Trained reflex demands we apply forward pressure on the yoke to quickly break the stall. Yet

Five Step Stall Recovery

1. Apply forward yoke pressure. To reduce angle of attack and get the wings safely flying again.

2. Apply full throttle. To increase windflow over the wing with prop blast.

3. Coordinate rudder and aileron to stop any turn. To prevent additional aerodynamic loading.

4. After recovery, establish an appropriate heading. Original heading or away from any hazard.

5. Climb at best-rate airspeed. To gain a safer altitude.

Figure 8-3
To best employ stall recovery techniques, pilots must first understand the reasons behind their control movements. Then they must train these moves to reflex action, triggered by the first indication of a stall.

natural instinct may shout, "Pull up! Get it away from the ground!" Your throttle hand has been trained to add power to get the plane flying again. Yet instinct may tell you to slow the action, reduce power. Many a good pilot has come to grief simply because panic let trained reflex succumb to natural instinct in a moment of crisis. Panic in a moment of crisis is your worst enemy. When flying an airplane, *force* yourself to keep thinking right through that moment.

Chapter 9

Return to Earth

An engine failure on takeoff can be merely critical, or a full-blown emergency. If the engine loses power during the roll or after rotation with plenty of stopping distance ahead, there is little trouble. If, however, the engine quits after liftoff with the airport already behind, the pilot often faces a truly desperate situation. Serious injury is a real prospect. After lowering the nose for airspeed, there is only time for the most meager of discrepancy checks (see Figure 9-1).

Then, the tough question: turn back to the airport or try for another spot? The answer is rarely clear cut. There are no firm guidelines to follow. This is because the situations are so varied: point and height of engine failure, airplane characteristics, partial or total power loss, nature of the airport and its surroundings. And too, there are so few pilots with personal experience to pass along; the event is a relatively rare occurrence.

Let me add here that I certainly am not experienced at making forced landings from takeoff. I have, however, conducted many simulated forced landings with pilots of all skill levels. I endeavor to keep these simulations as realistic as possible. But there remains a gap between realistic and real. How narrow or wide this gap is, I cannot say absolutely. Therefore, regard the comments that follow as circumstantial evidence. Weigh them against your own logic, and, if the ideas make sense, adopt them as your own.

There are some basic concepts for you to consider, which will improve your chances for a successful return to earth if a forced landing from takeoff should ever come your way. The nature of these basic concepts fall within two statements. First, know your airplane; second, know your airport.

Know Your Airplane

When must I land ahead and when do I have enough altitude to turn back? To a pilot facing a forced landing following takeoff, the answer lies in knowledge of the airplane. Most light planes will give *about* a mile of glide for each 1,000 feet of altitude.

Each 90° of turn usually costs *about* 250 feet. But only practical demonstration provides certainty for the plane you fly. Let's set up three rules of thumb. Then, let's have you modify them for the aircraft you fly. Conduct a trial, practical demonstration for each.

Brief Discrepancy Checks

- Confirm gear down

- Confirm electric fuel pump on

- Carburetor heat on

- Switch fuel tanks

- Switch fuel tanks

- Enrich mixture/advance throttle

- Try each magneto in turn

Figure 9-1
Quick-check emergency checklist.

Rule of Thumb 1

If the engine fails below 500 feet AGL, select the best area within 30° of turn and quarter-mile glide. To modify this rule for the plane you fly, conduct a practical demonstration. With an observer pilot on board to help spot traffic, fly to an airport with light traffic and long runway. Approach the runway threshold at a 30° angle. Slow your plane to a speed that simulates best rate of climb speed and descend so you reach the airport boundary about 400 feet AGL. As the runway nears, close your throttle and make a turn to short final. You will discover that even a shallow turn costs altitude. Modify rule number one to meet the capability of the plane you fly.

Rule of Thumb 2

If the engine fails between 500 and 1,000 feet AGL, select a landing spot that lies within a half mile and 90° of turn. To modify this rule for your airplane, conduct a practical demonstration. With an observer pilot aboard, fly to an uncongested airport with long runways. Approach your runway on base leg in slow flight at 500 feet AGL. Close the throttle as you approach final, a half-mile out. Turn toward the runway, gauge your plane's ability and modify rule two.

Rule of Thumb 3

If the engine fails above 1,000 feet AGL and the airport boundary lies within a half-mile, execute a turn and return to the field. This situation would occur, naturally, when departing a long runway, or when making a downwind departure. Again, with an observer pilot aboard and an uncongested airport beneath you, set up an exercise to modify this rule to the plane you fly. Overfly the runway at 1,000 feet AGL at a slow-flight speed which approximates climb speed. When the airport boundary is a half-mile behind, begin your simulated forced landing. Close the throttle, turn toward the airport, and decide if you could make it to an unobstructed area. Then, modify the rule to suit your airplane.

As you modify this rule, keep in mind the basic problem. Be careful your modified rule does not risk overreaching the capabilities of your plane.

Pilots who have attempted to turn back with insufficient altitude for the distance have either hit the ground while still in a turn or have tried to stretch the glide. Either is a setup for disaster. When a plane hits while turning, it usually catches a wing and cartwheels. A pilot who tries to stretch a glide often stalls, and a stall from even 50 feet is like falling off a four-story building. In either case, survival is doubtful.

Been There

Will your three rules of thumb provide the perfect solution for the actual forced landing you could someday encounter shortly after takeoff? Probably not. There are just too many variables. But, as you develop your rules, you see what you and your plane, as a team, can deliver in three representative situations (see Figure 9-2).

Keep these tentative plans filed in your memory as visualized actions based on your own observation and personal experience. And, should the occasion arise, you have in a sense "been there." Your memory has a good chance to trigger a workable solution.

Know Your Airport

You will probably never experience a forced landing from takeoff, but should it ever occur, chances are it will happen from the airport you use most — your home field. For this reason, study the departure paths with each takeoff. Survey those areas for possible landing sites. Conduct a similar survey of the airports you frequently visit and you eliminate a good measure of uncertainty from the unlikely event.

Worksheet: Forced Landing Following Takeoff

Modified Rule Of Thumb Number 1

If the engine fails below 500 AGL, select the best area that lies within _____ (distance) and 30 degrees of turn.

Modified Rule Of Thumb Number 2

If the engine fails between 500 and 1000 AGL, select the best area that lies within _____ (distance) and 90 degrees of turn.

Modified Rule Of Thumb Number 3

If the engine fails above 1000 AGL, and the airport boundary lies within _____ (distance), turn back to the field.

Figure 9-2
To a pilot facing a forced landing following takeoff, the answer lies in knowledge of the airplane.

When you enter the pattern of an unfamiliar airport, remind yourself that you will soon be departing. So while on the downwind leg, survey the departure path for likely spots. Then, should the engine fail on departure when a turn-back is inadvisable, you will have an idea where relative safety lies.

Someday you may need to land where **no** safety lies. Even the big-city airport usually offers a possible emergency site — a parking lot, expressway, or lake. But occasionally there is nothing. You must then land where you cannot land.

No Landable Patch of Survival in Sight

If this nightmare should ever come my way, logic will tell me two things: First, at the very least I'm going to get hurt. Second, even though the engine may be dead, the rest of the plane certainly is not. I will still have elevators, ailerons, rudder, and flaps. I will use that control as well as I can to come out alive. I will put a three-part landing procedure into play.

1. Aim for a spot that will let me avoid hitting anything solid with the nose. I don't care about the rest of the plane, but I want to keep the cabin more or less intact.

2. Approach will be at the slowest possible impact speed; full flaps. Yet, I will not let those wings stall; I don't want to fall that last 50 feet.

3. I will not throw in the towel. Even if it continues to look hopeless, I will keep working right up to the last moment, even into that last moment, because the deciding factor may lie within that last instant of control. So often, lessons of the sky apply also to living life.

Hopelessness and Hope

Picture yourself in your plane and in this situation: Your engine quit seconds ago at 400 feet AGL with the airport well behind and nothing but a busy mid-morning city beneath. You've turned toward the only opening you could find — a wide street in a business area. Now, at 100 feet and lined up with the street, you easily see the lamp posts bordering your landing area, the power lines stretched across each corner, delivery vans, cars, people. You hold a straight approach path with ailerons and rudder, vaguely realizing you're gripping the yoke with both hands, elbows locked straight. A rear seat passenger is trying to say something but she might as well be speaking a foreign tongue; all your concentration is straight ahead. On either side, walls of brick, cement and windows are rising above you, the windmilling prop cuts through the first web of power lines with a blue flash, and your plane's nose is down in an attempt to maintain approach speed. Beyond the windscreen are people, some frozen looking up, some running, others unaware of what is about to happen. You're aware that all three passengers, even the kid, are yanking about now, screaming. You lift the nose for the round-out and an oncoming Chevrolet jumps the curb, more power lines pass overhead, and your projected landing path points to an intersection filled with a steady flow of traffic crossing on the green.

It is at this point of crisis you must try your very hardest. You cannot give up; you must keep working and thinking right up to the last moment, even into that moment. Because your final instant of airmanship could very well be the deciding factor (see Figure 9-3).

Cardinal Rules

Establish a safe glide speed.

Do not even hope to overreach your plane's demonstrated capability.

Maintain airspeed and directional control with still-functioning elevators, ailerons, rudder, and flaps.

Reduce speed to the slowest safe approach speed.

Do not allow the wings to stall prior to touchdown or impact.

Avoid touching down while in a turn.

Avoid hitting anything solid with the nose.

Never throw in the towel; keep working and thinking.

Figure 9-3
Engine failure on takeoff: crisis management.

Chapter 10

Off and Safely Away

Takeoff is the most critical phase of a normal flight. It's the time and place for a preponderance of flying accidents. Yet, many pilots who work hard to deliver are-we-down-yet landings often just push the throttle and hope to get it off before anything goes wrong.

There are two basic reasons that make takeoffs more critical than landings. First, there are factors surrounding both maneuvers that impede a takeoff far more than they do a landing — simple gravity, for example. In a landing we're coming down anyway. (In all of recorded aviation history, we haven't yet gotten a plane stuck up there.) But on takeoff, gravity fights every inch of altitude. We had better be in an optimally performing airplane, using good pilot technique.

Second, a tried pilot, a true airplane. A landing has a pilot aboard with very recent flight experience, an hour or so at the controls. But let's face it. We don't fly as often as we'd like. The pilot at the helm on takeoff may not have touched those controls for days, weeks, or (gulp!) months. The plane is in much the same situation — already proven a true ship for the past hour or so. But at takeoff it is untested. Will it perform with the capability needed? Only an aware pilot using good pilot technique can tell for sure.

Once astride the center stripes, with the nosewheel aimed straight ahead, put your good pilot technique into play. Think of your takeoff as three separate maneuvers: the takeoff run, liftoff, and initial climbout.

Making the Takeoff Run

The takeoff run asks you for three precise actions: the most rapid acceleration possible to rotate speed, positive directional control, crosswind correction.

Acceleration

A smooth hand on the throttle is the first step toward rapid acceleration. Too quickly is likely to feed fuel faster than cylinders can digest it; the engine will falter and significantly reduce acceleration. Best power application has you smoothly advancing throttle as fast as the engine can take it without giving audible sounds of misfire.

Once you apply full throttle, glance at the tachometer. Is the engine performing 100%, or does anemic power indication suggest an abort?

Deflected control surfaces add considerable drag as speed increases on the takeoff run. Allow control surfaces to streamline unless there is reason to move them, such as crosswind correction. Some pilots develop a habit of "walking" the rudder for directional control. Not only is this an ineffective way to keep the plane going straight, but each wiggle of that rudder adds drag to slow the action.

Some pilots feel they can assist acceleration by lifting weight from the nosewheel as soon as ground speed permits. Their thinking is to reduce rolling friction. But by increasing angle of attack, they create lift, which in turn creates aerodynamic drag. Acceleration is actually impaired. Conversely, do not press the yoke forward. This creates undue rolling friction and may create serious directional problems. Best to let control surfaces streamline unless there's a real need that takes precedence over acceleration.

Directional Control

Rudder and steerable nosewheel are the principle tools of directional control during the takeoff run; to keep brakes out of the steering action, keep your heels on the floor. During your takeoff run, **slipstream effect** tries to slew your plane to the left. Slipstream effect occurs as prop wash corkscrews around the fuselage to strike the left side of the vertical tailplane. It's most apparent when you first apply power. Just anticipate the occurrence and apply slight right rudder to stay astride the centerline.

Directional control during the run is easily disturbed by aileron drag (also called adverse yaw); when you turn the control wheel in one direction, the airplane turns in the opposite direction. Turn the wheel to the right, say, and the right aileron lifts to be shielded from the wind flow by the wing's upper curved surface. The left aileron dips below the wing into the wind and the plane slews left.

A problem arises should the pilot try to correct a swerve by instinctively turning the yoke away from the swerve; a reversion to a car's steering wheel. But this action further intensifies the swerve with aileron drag. The proper action, naturally, would have been to correct with rudder and nosewheel steering.

Crosswind Correction

Your primary defense against a crosswind during the takeoff run is the positive use of aileron drag. Let's say a crosswind blows from the left. Turn the control wheel in that direction and the right aileron digs down into the onrushing air. Now the crosswind against the vertical stabilizer tries to swing the plane left, but aileron drag counters to the right to keep the plane on centerline (see Figure 10-1).

How much aileron to use? Well, it's practically impossible to use too much as the takeoff roll begins. Initial ground speed is so slow, the down aileron produces only minimal drag. So, begin the roll with full deflection into the crosswind. Two things happen as

Figure 10-1
With wind blowing from the left, right aileron drag counters the crosswind to keep the plane on the centerline.

ground speed increases. First, drag increases with speed. Second, a crosswind doesn't affect a faster-moving plane as much as a slower one, a condition of time and force. So, as your plane accelerates, start decreasing aileron. Time this decrease so full deflection reduces to near-zero aileron just as you lift off.

Each make and model has a maximum crosswind component it can safely accept. There's a limit beyond which there's just not enough aileron drag to do the job. This maximum crosswind component is usually stated in the plane's manual; often about one-third of stall speed.

Lifting Off

The liftoff maneuver of the takeoff sequence asks you to perform two primary duties during the segment's short duration: precisely control airspeed and accurately control direction by correcting for crosswind and P-factor.

Airspeed Control

If you try to lift off before the wings are ready to fly, you lengthen the takeoff distance and create directional problems. Try to hold the plane ground-bound too long and again distance and control suffer. Adhere to your manual's recommended rotate speed.

Directional Control

Two primary forces try to impair directional control at liftoff: crosswind and P-factor. You have reduced aileron deflection to near zero at the moment of liftoff, yet the crosswind still exists. So, as the wheels leave the runway, make a slight, coordinated turn to establish a crab into the wind. (At a typical liftoff speed of 55-60 knots, you will correct about 1° for each knot of direct, crosswind component.)

P-factor comes from the propeller's motion when the plane is pitched for liftoff. The plane tends to swing left, so anticipate and be ready with right rudder pressure to keep yourself dead on centerline.

Flying the Initial Climbout

The initial climbout maneuver of your takeoff sequence asks for three principle elements of good pilot technique: airspeed control, directional control, and traffic avoidance.

Airspeed Control

Your plane will continue to accelerate from liftoff. If you're holding pitch attitude that produces best-rate-of-climb speed (determined from practiced experience), the plane will settle to this speed about 50 feet above the ground. Once the airspeed indicator hits best-rate speed, retrim to hold it.

If your takeoff employed flaps, start retracting them, one increment at a time, retrimming to hold your speed with each retraction. Pilots who "dump" all the flaps after liftoff find a constant airspeed is almost impossible to maintain. They may also suffer an actual loss of altitude on the initial climbout, or bring their plane dangerously close to its flaps-up stall speed.

Once best-rate-of-climb speed is well established, raise the gear if you're flying a retractable. Watch the airspeed indicator as you do, move the nose to keep airspeed captured, then retrim. It's a good idea to delay retraction until this time. Pilots who quickly retract after liftoff and find the need to get back on the ground could forget to lower the gear again in their excitement.

Directional Control

Again, crosswind and the left-turning tendency of P-factor try to move you off course. (The wind correction angle which held course after liftoff will likely hold the course through the few hundred feet of initial climbout. True, the plane's speed increases steadily during this time, but the crosswind's velocity also increases with each yard of altitude.)

Stay astride the centerline as long as the runway appears ahead of you. Before the runway disappears from sight, pick out two landmarks straight ahead to help keep runway alignment. If you let your plane drift, you may find an obstacle, or that your pattern exit turn places you directly in front of a faster plane departing behind you (see Figure 10-2).

Traffic Avoidance

Maintain an alert traffic watch during initial climbout. An airport's close vicinity is a crowded place, often with pilots distracted by arrival and departure procedures. Let your efforts follow two lines: spotting other planes and making yourself more visible to other pilots.

When you look for planes, search that band of sky three inches above and below the horizon and scan each 30° sector of sky. (You may need to dip the nose for a look ahead.) After turning your head toward each sector, move your eyes rather than your head for an unblurred look. And remember, your eyes work like a telescope;

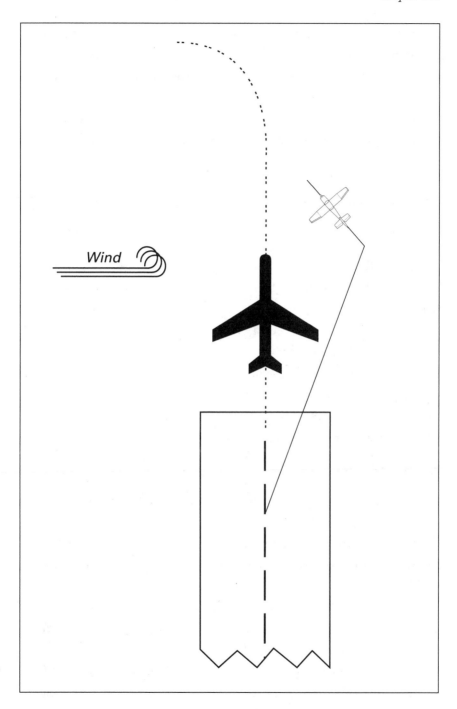

Figure 10-2
Uncorrected drift may place you in the path of a faster plane departing behind you.

you must vary your range of focus. We tend to focus only out to the horizon — and look right through a nearby plane.

Once away from the runway, do everything possible to protect yourself from *unseen* traffic; alert them to you. For example, keep your landing light blazing while in the traffic area. You may not see head-on traffic (the toughest of all to spot), but they should certainly see you. By the same token, turn your strobes on — quite visible even during daylight. And by all means depart with your transponder on. A controller will see your blip and warn participating traffic of your presence even if you are not in touch with ATC.

Think of your takeoff as three maneuvers: takeoff run, liftoff, initial climbout. Perform each with good, methodical pilot technique and you will deliver a safe takeoff with each flight.

Cardinal Rules for Takeoff Safety

If you asked me to state just 10 pilot actions critical to takeoff safety, I'd list:

1. Know and follow your aircraft manual's takeoff recommendations. The manufacturer knows what works best for its airplane and states tried and proven procedures with the prime intent to keep you within your plane's operating design limits. Operate your plane within these limits and it will perform as the manufacturer predicts. Operate beyond these design limits, and no one knows what to expect.

2. Evaluate the overall situation at hand and relate it to your plane's takeoff performance rate of climb, and loading charts. Don't rely on past successes; each takeoff must stand on its own. Remember, as you use your charts, they must relate to the *real world* you face on takeoff. Be ready to modify the charts' values to meet the uncharted values which challenge your takeoff — the

higher-than-50 foot obstacle, a very soft surface, a slight tailwind on a one-way strip, a needed rate of climb inconsistent with your load of the day — all the variables of the real world. And by all means, run a weight and balance calculation anytime there is the slightest reason for concern.

3. Know what you and your plane, as a team, can deliver. Once you know your plane's capabilities through a study of your manual's charts and recommended procedures, you have half the equation. The other half rests in knowledge of your abilities to match the plane's performance. Questions may arise which need answers. For instance, if obstacle clearance is critical, can I pin down best-angle climb speed and hold it there, or, how much crosswind can I handle? When facing a critical takeoff it's important to know, from demonstrated performance, your own limitations and not depend on a skill that just isn't there. As Zane Grey, the western writer, so often advised, "Never face down seven when all you're packin' is a six-shooter."

4. Allow an adequate safety margin of runway length. The unforeseen can happen — an unexpected up-slope, a rough spot in the turf runway, or simple bad math applied to a performance chart. After calculating your required runway length against the chart, allow another 50% for a safety margin.

5. Plan an abort point before you take the runway. If you do not already hold the decision to abort if necessary, you may be subconsciously committed to "press on regardless" when things start going wrong. When preparing to takeoff, hold in mind your primary plan to abort. Then, if you reach your abort point with

everything going fine, put your secondary plan into play — complete your takeoff.

6. Have in mind an emergency landing area. The worst time for an emergency landing to come your way is during those first few hundred feet of altitude following liftoff. So before a departure from your home airport, know from previous flights where relative safety lies. And when approaching downwind at an unfamiliar airport, scout out a likely area which will give a measure of safety to your later departure.

7. Never take a defective plane to the air. I know this sounds simplistic, but it happens very often and with great regularity. Your attitude toward the preflight inspection is critical. All too often pilots conduct a preflight with the preconceived notion that the plane is probably OK. The pilot who begins preflighting only 10 minutes prior to planned departure time is a good example of this. That pilot obviously does not *expect* to find anything wrong which may require a second opinion, service or repair. And since that pilot *expects* to find nothing, discrepancies are bound to slip past. Be highly suspicious of your aircraft. Let stubbornness work you through the checklist to ferret out any hidden hazards.

8. Keep your eyes on the road during taxi and takeoff. Should you look down within the cockpit while moving — to set frequencies, for example, or to reach for a chart lying on the back seat — you run the risk of hitting something, or at the very least, swerving. Loss of directional control on the ground is a major, major producer of airplane accidents. And pilot inattentiveness in a moving plane often alerts Fate that a potential victim lies close at hand.

9. Make every takeoff a practice takeoff. It's easy to do. As you prepare to takeoff, methodically adhere to your written checklists. Taxi to the centerline and make your takeoff run with the nosewheel rolling exactly along the stripes. Rotate at the precise recommended speed and hit best-rate-of-climb right on the mark. Absolutely kill wind drift with headings you deliberately choose, and execute a perfect pattern exit. The accuracy and finesse you develop through constant practice with each normal takeoff gives you a reserve of competence you may someday need to face the abnormal departure.

10. Deliver a 100% effort with each takeoff. Safe takeoffs don't just happen. This 100% effort begins long before you have the throttle in hand. As you research conditions, evaluate your own skill and make sure your plane is up to the task. Maximum effort here means you know the factors that influence takeoffs, you have learned your plane's capabilities and you have developed your skill to control that capability. With each departure, in fact, you have a total awareness of the environment, the airplane, and yourself. Make a commitment to that degree of effort and you will not fail to deliver a safe departure each time you fly.

Part III

En Route

*T*he airplane has unveiled for us
the true face of the earth.

Antoine de Saint Exupery, *Wind, Sand and Stars*

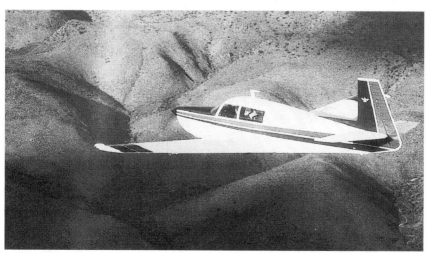

Photo courtesy of Mooney Aircraft, Inc.

Chapter 11

Low-Altitude Flying

The '70s found me overflying Florida's wilderness areas as a wildlife survey pilot, serving a study of the bald eagle. Decades of land development and widespread pesticide use had finally caught up with the eagle's ability to survive; its reduced numbers were in rapid decline.

The survey's task was to help find solutions which could co-exist with the needs of a rapidly expanding human population. A survey by small plane was decided upon as the best way to reach the state's inaccessible areas and give naturalists a close look directly into nests during the incubation, hatching and fledging processes. A small, throttled-down engine did not disturb the eagles.

You would have enjoyed those flights, especially the Everglades. Once into their midst, not a mark of civilization. There, creeping along with low power at survey height you could have seen, from horizon to horizon, just what Earth was like before humans took over. Its unbroken expanse of head-high grasslands, hardwood hammocks, low-lying mangroves and meandering, shifting waterways gave hands-on definition to the term primeval.

My favorite of the survey was a small patch of pristine wilderness of only several hundred acres. It lay just a few miles south of the swiftly accelerating growth of the metropolitan Orlando complex. A crystalline, winding, spring-fed river ran through it. Along its banks towered huge gray-trunked bald cypress that were already giants before Columbus sailed, and stands of emerald-crowned long-leaf pines, many holding ancient bromeliads the size of my small plane's cockpit. Long beards of Spanish moss swaying from century-old live oaks gave gray-green backdrops to low-flying white wood storks and ibis, each with wingspans equal to the plane's horizontal stabilizer. And, of course, there were eagles.

It was an Eden, but one with a discordant note. By pointing the nose northward and lifting the plane a few extra feet you could see the tops of derricks, cranes, and high-rise superstructures a scant 10 miles away, steadily working southward. Had you been along you would have felt the unease, too; seeing first-hand a small piece of Earth running out of time.

As you might imagine, these survey flights were conducted at low altitude. There is no phrase to describe low-altitude flying other than "risky business." In the case of these flights both naturalist and pilot aboard knew the magnitude of this risk and through lengthy discussions each had made the decision to assume the personal risk in order to serve the purpose; populated areas were avoided. Then, once aloft, every action and thought was directed toward recognizing and minimizing this risk. I make these statements to emphasize that neither I nor anyone else condone low flying as either a safe or normal procedure. Low flying can place pilot, passengers and those below at life-threatening risk.

It is possible, however, that circumstances may someday converge on a flight in such a manner that forces a pilot to fly uncomfortably close to the ground. Then, basic precautions, which evolved from the wildlife survey flights, may help you minimize low-altitude hazards.

Low-Flight Precautions

By the time you might find yourself flying within 1,500 feet AGL to stay out of clouds, you should be at an alternate airport in a position to land. But it may sometime happen that you find yourself at low altitude with no runway in sight. Flawed judgement, bad information, or the capriciousness of the weather itself can throw plane and pilot into that predicament. Several simple pilot actions will help relieve the risks (see Figure 11-1).

Reduce Airspeed

When pressed low to the ground you can find some reassurance in knowing that lowering clouds rarely come down right to the surface as long as you maneuver to stay clear of any precip. Ridges and obstacles, however, can easily rise to close the gap between cloud and collision. Your first defense against such a collision is simply to slow down.

A speed produced by 55% power is appropriate to most light aircraft; somewhat slower if visibility is restricted. Things happen quickly at low altitude. A flight path that seems clear one minute might have an obstacle in it the next. The slower speed often lets a momentary inattention pass without harm; it gives the pilot extra reaction time, as well as better maneuverability by virtue of a shorter turning radius.

Carburetor heat

Run with the carburetor heat full hot. The high humidity often present in low-altitude flying, as well as the slow-turning engine, are very apt to produce carburetor ice. Frequent power changes may prevent early detection and your first warning could be a sputtering engine. (Just remember to adjust your fuel flow against the over-rich mixture that carburetor heat imposes.)

Fuel Pump, Tanks, and Flaps

If ever forced to fly within 1,500 feet AGL, turn on your electric fuel pump, switch to the fullest tank, and lower flaps one notch. A malfunction in the engine-driven fuel pump can

Precautions to Help Relieve Hazards

Reduce your airspeed.

Apply carburetor heat.

Turn on the electric fuel pump.

Switch to the fullest tank.

Lower one notch of flaps.

Keep a hand on the throttle.

Avoid making steep turns.

When possible, make evasive turns into the wind.

Keep your plane properly trimmed.

Draw your course on the chart and maintain an awareness of position.

Fly with the landing light and strobe on. Maintain a careful traffic watch.

Maintain radio contact with a ground facility.

Figure 11-1
These precautionary actions will not make a safe procedure of low flying. They will simply help make the best of a bad situation.

cause a momentary loss of power that is unaffordable at low altitude. Switching to the fat tank at the outset of the low flight can prevent a busy pilot's forgetfulness from turning into an accident. One notch of flaps increases the margin between flying speed and stalling speed should a quick turn away from a ridge or obstacle become necessary, yet doesn't greatly affect the plane's performance.

I know that fuel pumps rarely fail, that we would never run a tank dry, or inadvertently stall the plane. What we're talking about here is protecting against the unimaginable. But during low-altitude flying, strange things just seem to happen.

Hand on the Throttle

Keep a hand on the throttle and add a touch of power should you need to turn away from a hazard. This action reduces the plane's stall speed during the brief period of increased load factor, and helps prevent an unintentional loss of altitude in the turn.

Avoid steep turns in excess of 30° banks. This, of course, is to prevent high load factors that could induce a stall.

Remain aware of wind direction when avoiding obstacles. When possible, turn your evasive maneuver into the wind. Wind drift is significant during low-altitude turns and you could easily fly into a second, unseen obstacle. This is particularly important in high-wing models, which hide a pilot's view during the turn.

Keep the plane in proper trim; retrim with each change of power or flaps. Attitude control is all-important at low altitude. Either an unintended nose up or nose down can spell disaster for a pilot whose attentions are distracted. And out-of-trim airplanes practically beg their pilots to let attentions wander.

Lights On

The circumstances which forced you to fly low may also be affecting other flights. If so, you may not be alone in that narrow band of airspace. Turn on your landing and strobe lights to help avert a possible midair.

Even through your cockpit workload might be heavy, maintain a constant vigil for traffic. Scan especially, that band of airspace three inches above and below the horizon — the place most colliding aircraft fly from.

Careful Navigation

Draw your course on the chart with a heavy line. This anticipates a strong reliance on pilotage (navigation by landmarks) should you drop below VOR reception range. To further aid pilotage navigation, circle prominent landmarks at estimated ten minute intervals along the route. Choose landmarks that will stand out even in the poor perspective of low-altitude flying. Large or tall landmarks, such as towns, bodies of water, or antenna farms are easier to see than roads, streams or railways, when the going gets low.

It takes concentration and effort to keep a minute-by-minute track of your position when flying low. But the moment you become uncertain of where you are, is the moment things tend to take a turn for the worse. And racing lowering clouds to the ground is no fun when you don't know which way it is to the finish line.

Maintain Communications

A pilot forced by circumstances to fly within 1,500 feet AGL should stay in constant contact with a ground facility. The problem here is selecting a station in range. (Perhaps 25 miles at several hundred feet with a typical light plane radio.) Your best bet might be the 121.5 emergency frequency. While your sectional chart may not show a primary facility within hearing distance, chances are that an ATC remote outlet is nearby to receive your call.

You do not need to declare an emergency to contact a facility with 121.5. Just tell them of your situation, that you're concerned, and ask them to stick with you; they will. The people on the ground cannot fly the plane or make decisions, true. But they can provide information to a pilot who might be quickly running out of options. The point is this: alert your ground support system *before* your situation becomes an emergency. Once a situation deteriorates into a real emergency, your options are usually so limited that advice and support from the ground is of minimal value.

These several suggestions will not make a safe procedure of low flight — there is no way to do that. But they will help stack the deck toward your favor until you can fly yourself out of the unwanted situation.

Epilog

A few results of the wildlife survey twenty years after: Florida's mature bald eagle population has tripled; hatchlings are up four-fold. And that patch of Eden (along with other areas of habitat) has been assured of permanent protection through the Land Mitigation program. There is satisfaction to be found in looking back to discover your efforts have played a small hand in a worthwhile venture.

Chapter 12

Open Door Policy and Other Unexpected Encounters

For most pilots, one true delight of flight lies within the potential each hour aloft holds for an unexpected encounter. Not a life-threatening or plane-damaging emergency, mind you; no pilot wants that. But rather a simple element of the flight suddenly gone wrong; a challenge from plane or sky which tests our ability to put the situation right — adventure.

The thought of this potential encounter plays through the back canyons of your mind with every takeoff you make. Will this flight hold the test? Will my ability answer that test? Thus, every takeoff in turn brings the call of first-born adventure, no matter how long you have been at flying. And make no mistake, you *do* seek adventure. Otherwise you would never have been drawn to the cockpit which offers no guarantees.

Here are a few potential unexpected encounters to enjoy, first as you read along and, second, if good luck is with you, from behind the controls.

Open Door Policy

There is one unexpected encounter that sooner or later nearly every pilot faces. Not a critical situation, really, unless the pilot chooses to make it so. Sooner or later nearly every pilot has a door pop open during the takeoff run or initial climb-out. Nothing bad happens in a typical lightplane. But it is noisy! POW!

WHooooSH! The noise alone can spook an uninformed pilot into error. But flight characteristics remain virtually unaffected. The door just trails open two inches or so and no one can push hard enough to fall out. Only a minor annoyance, really, but not all pilots know that. A story? Sure. Draw your chair closer and I'll tell you exactly what happened.

The story is not new, you've heard it before because unfortunately nearly every airport has had a similar experience. Ian was the embodiment of every Irish ballad ever written. He stood five feet five inches and had a happy-go-lucky grin just as wide. With a shock of red hair and a gift of blarney, he had a ready friendship for all. Ian was (and remained) a good pilot.

A score-and-a-half years ago, Ian bought a nearly new, sleek, four-place retractable of 260 HP. State of the art. And it was indeed art — soft smoke-blue with burgundy striping, latest stuff stacked in the panel, genuine leather interior. It was the star of the ramp. Ian was proud; we all were proud.

Ian had just completed an hour's checkout in the craft and was ready for a solo hop. We watched him taxi out, discussing the marvelous deep-throated power, just how that funny tail really worked — stuff like that.

In the cockpit, at runway's end, Ian shoved in takeoff power. The acceleration, the crisp liftoff. Then, POW! WHooooSH! Ian stiffened like a corpse. That tornado of wind pouring in just *had* to blow his ship apart! He *had* to get it down, right now! But there wasn't enough runway left under him. Fortunately (or unfortunately) big Lake Barton was dead ahead.

Well, you guessed it. Even from the hangar, we could see and hear that terrible splash. Ian was a good swimmer, but that beautiful ship sank like a punctured rubber raft.

If this unexpected encounter should ever come your way, treat it as a minor mishap. You have three easy options, depending on whether or not you are still on the runway when the door opens. If the door pops during your ground run with plenty of stopping distance ahead, the solution is simple. First, out of courtesy, quickly reassure your passenger; "It's OK. Nothing will happen." Then, throttle back, exit the runway, close and *lock* the door, and grumble your way back for a second run while you try to convince your stone-faced passenger to stay aboard for another go.

If the door opens after liftoff or with inadequate stopping distance ahead, continue with the takeoff. Then you have two options. You can either circle and land to close the door, or climb to cruise altitude and do it there. The point is, don't wrestle with the door at low altitude. During those distracted moments you could fly right into something, or allow the stall attitude to happen. If you choose to climb to altitude with the door sprung open, nothing bad will happen. (If it's the right-hand door, however, your passenger may tend to gurgle a bit now and then. But that aside, the climb will be uneventful.) Cabin doors are sometimes difficult to close in flight. It will help relieve the pressures against it if you slow-fly and open a window or storm vent.

If either the baggage or cowl hatch opens in flight, you have only one option. You can't reach either from your position, and *don't even ask* your passenger to unstrap and crawl back to close the howling baggage hatch. You must return for a landing.

If it's the cowl hatch that's in question, you may have another minor annoyance as you return for landing. The slipstream may flutter the hatch door hard enough to do damage. If this happens, fly your plane in a *slight* slip to alter the slipstream. A few seconds with aileron and rudder produces the right combination that lets the hatch lie flat. No problem.

As I said, Ian's unfortunate flight occurred many years ago. He never had another mishap. Some time ago, at the insistence of his loving family, Ian, at age seventy-six, gave up flying. I think it was a wise decision. Slainthe Is Saol Agat, Ian!

Other Unexpected Encounters

Before discussing specific malfunctions, let's list the few things you should do ***anytime*** a situation of concern comes your way:

1. If conditions and time permit, climb to a higher altitude. Not only will you increase your communications range, but with many potential problems, extra altitude is like having extra money in the bank.

2. Estimate the time you can remain aloft. Remaining fuel is a factor, as is the nature of your plane's malfunction. (A rough engine will usually get you home, for example, but rapidly falling oil pressure is another matter.) Plan to have your injured bird at roost before dark.

3. Communicate with an FAA facility. Any facility will do the job. If you are already working a frequency, then stay on it. If you are unsure of a working frequency, go to the emergency 121.5. That's what it's there for, all FAA facilities monitor it, and your position is automatically plotted when calling on 121.5. Remember, you don't need to declare an emergency to use 121.5. Quite the contrary, it's important to alert your ground support system *before* your situation becomes an emergency. In fact, once a situation deteriorates into a real emergency, your options are often so limited that advice and support from the ground is of minimal value. In general, you should put out a call of concern any time:

   a. your fuel supply first comes into question,

   b. you become unsure of your position,

   c. an equipment malfunction arises for which you cannot effect an immediate fix,

   d. you feel you are "coming down with something," like flu, which may impair you, or

   e. weather starts to look a bit scary — certainly before clouds force you below 2,000 feet AGL, visibility

drops below five miles, or it looks like you may be
forced to enter precip, or fly above a significant
cloud layer.

Again, you do not need to declare an emergency to get
help. Just tell someone you have a concern and ask them
to stick with you. They will. When you ask for
assistance, make a few standard requests.

  a. A radar or direction finding (DF) confirmation of
your present position.

  b. The heading and estimated time enroute to an
appropriate alternate airport.

  c. Advice in selecting an appropriate airport. If your
concern is a misfiring engine, for example, you will
want to land at an airport with maintenance
facilities. Or, if your problem suggests a hazardous
landing (like a gear-up), you will want an airport
with fire and rescue equipment.

4. If finding the remedy to a mechanical problem
confounds you, put in a call to a nearby FBO's unicom.
Ask to speak to their mechanic.

5. Finally, make sure your passengers know the situation.
The last thing a pilot wants is panicky passengers.
When given the facts, however, most passengers will
cooperate with a degree of calm. Just tell them of the
problem, reassure them that ground assistance has been
alerted, you have plans for a safe arrival and you can
cope. Handle it right and your passengers will relish
retelling the adventure over their supper tables for
months to come.

Rough-Running Engine

The most common equipment problem you may expect to
encounter is a rough-running engine. This rarely develops into a

serious problem. Lightplane engines are pretty reliable and will most often keep you flying until you can either effect a remedy or reach a suitable airport for repair.

Common causes for a rough-running engine are a loss of adequate fuel flow, carburetor ice, or improper ignition. A simple checklist usually provides the fix:

1. Throttle — restore cruise power.
2. Fuel selector — switch tanks.
3. Auxiliary fuel pump — on.
4. Carburetor heat — full on.
5. Mixture — full rich, then lean.
6. Magnetos — check each, return to BOTH.
7. Use smoothest throttle, mixture, mags.

In-Flight Engine Restarts

The two most common reasons for inadvertently killing an engine in flight are running a tank dry and pulling the mixture control when all you really wanted to do was apply carburetor heat. To protect the engine from a sudden burst of power as you refire the motor, follow a logical restart procedure:

1. Throttle — retard.
2. Fuel selector — switch tanks.
3. Mixture control — full rich.
4. Fuel pump — on.
5. Restart engine — windmilling prop/starter, as needed.
6. After restart — fuel pump off, reposition throttle and mixture.

Overheating Engine

Engine overheating in flight is most often caused by restricted airflow across the cylinders, a too-lean fuel mixture, or a prolonged climb at improper power settings or airspeed. Take three steps to bring the temperature gauge down:

1. Enrich the fuel mixture.
2. Open the cowl flaps.
3. Fly level at 55% power.

Runaway or Inoperative Electric Trim

If an electric trim control should either run beyond your control, or does not move at all, use a checklist:

1. Aircraft attitude — physically hold enough control pressure that overrides adverse trim to maintain proper attitude.
2. Deactivate trim system — pull circuit breaker or fuse, trim switch off.
3. Retrim — use manual trim control.
4. Electric trim circuit — leave inoperative until repaired.

Electrical System Overload

Some ammeters display the electrical load on the alternator. Others show whether the battery is charging or discharging. Review your plane's flight manual to determine the normal indication. Many light airplanes are also equipped with a circuit overload warning light. Should this warning light illuminate in flight, switch off the entire master switch for several seconds to allow the alternator to reset. If the overload condition does not reoccur when the master switch is turned back on, continue your flight.

If, on the other hand, the warning light returns, an alternator malfunction is likely. In this case, turn off either the entire master switch or, if provided, the separate alternator half. Head for a convenient airport with maintenance facilities since the airplane's electrical needs may drain the battery. Don't worry about the engine quitting even if you do drain the battery. Aircraft engines — unlike automobiles — receive their firing power from the magnetos, not the battery.

Falling Oil Pressure

If you note a substantial reduction of oil pressure in flight, look at the oil *temperature* gauge to analyze the situation. If oil temperature remains normal, the malfunction most probably lies in the oil pressure gauge itself. In this case, maintain normal engine power, remain alert, and divert to a suitable airport to evaluate the source of trouble.

If, however, the oil pressure gauge shows near-zero pressure, accompanied by high oil temperature, you must anticipate imminent engine failure. Reduce power to below 55% and use the power that remains to reach a close by, suitable landing area.

Manual Landing Gear Extension

Be aware that some planes place the emergency manual extension handle in an inconvenient position. Do not let this inconvenience deter you from looking for traffic as you work with the crank. A midair could render your gear extension labors totally useless.

Should your electric landing gear motor provide you with an unexpected encounter, apply a short checklist:

1. Landing gear switch — down.
2. Altitude — 2,000 feet AGL minimum if conditions permit.
3. Landing gear motor — deactivate by pulling circuit breaker or fuse. (Inspect fuse for possible replacement.)
4. Airspeed — reduce to gear extension speed.
5. Manually extend gear — aircraft flight manual procedure.
6. After landing — leave gear-motor circuit inoperative, leave gear switch down.

While manually extending an electric gear is an approved procedure, manually *retracting* the gear is not. If, after takeoff, the landing gear does not come up with the gear switch, something is obviously wrong. Return the switch to DOWN and leave the gear extended until you can land and get the thing fixed.

The Golden Rules

If you asked me to state only three golden rules for handling a malfunction aloft, I'd list:

1. Communicate with the ground at your first feeling of real concern, *before* the situation becomes an emergency.
2. Know your plane's flight manual as well as you know the lyrics to your favorite song. Keep the manual aboard. Most modern flight manuals suggest remedies for the most common malfunctions.
3. Level with your passengers. Tell them the nature of the problem and what you intend to do about it.

Epilog

Adventure need not be an act of daring-do. In truth, high adventure is anything you *wish* to call high adventure while you are doing it. Adventure is so important to a full life, and the potential for the unexpected encounter surrounds you in every waking moment if you only reach for it. To best discover the waiting adventure lying nearby, apply a rule of thumb: short of actual rudeness, make every good attempt to avoid the company of those who insist upon being dull.

Chapter 13

Improving Communications With ATC

Compliance with regulations and standard operating procedures give order to our airspace and lend safety to our flights. Compliance helps assure each pilot aloft everyone is in the right place at the right time doing the right thing; we know what to expect from one another.

However, as many elements of compliance are put into action, they first must pass through a common funnel: air to ground radio communications. With proper and comprehended communications, the system flows smoothly; poor communications cause breaks in this flow and often hold potential for mishap.

There are three ATC facilities with which nearly every pilot communicates during most cross-country flights: flight service station, tower control, and approach/departure control. Based on conversations with controllers and FSS specialists, here are a few thoughts on the use of each.

Flight Service Station

Flight Service Stations (FSS) are FAA facilities that supply enroute pilots with virtually any aeronautical information they require, provide answers and solutions to those flights in need of special assistance, and broadcast weather advisories. They receive and process flight plans, and give pilot weather and route briefings. FSS is the principle enroute communications provider for VFR aircraft.

A senior FSS specialist (the voice you hear over your radio) asked that we be reminded their middle name is "service." Think of FSS as your traveling encyclopedia. They do have answers for most needs — be it a frequency to provide radar services, length of the wind-favored runway or density altitude at destination, assisting with a DVFR, and the myriad of other answers which make your flight easier, safer and more enjoyable. Never hesitate to call with a question or concern; FSS specialists are able and happy to help.

Special Assistance

Should distress or uncertainty ever climb into your cockpit, FSS is your logical first point of contact for assistance. If you are already working a FSS frequency (and as a VFR flight, you should be most of the time) then stay on it. If you are unsure of a working frequency, go to the emergency 121.5 — that's what it's there for, nearly all FSS outlets monitor it, and someone will answer you.

Remember, you don't need to declare an emergency to use 121.5. Quite the contrary. It's important that you alert FSS *before* your situation becomes an emergency. In general, you should put out a call of concern anytime

1. your fuel supply first comes into question,
2. you become unsure of your position,
3. an equipment malfunction arises for which you cannot effect an immediate fix, or
4. weather starts to look a bit scary.

Just tell FSS you have a concern and ask them to stick with you. They will.

Common FSS Communication Errors

FSS specialists handling in-flight pilot needs note a few common communications errors that impede their efforts to render good service. The most common of all occurs on initial contact: many pilots fail to state their listening frequency. Standard procedure has pilots giving call signs and the frequency they are listening to, then waiting for a FSS reply before further transmitting: "Macon radio. Piper 4531 Charlie, listening 122.2."

FSS specialists work communication panels of two dozen or more frequencies. The specialist may not be looking at the panel to see the frequency light blink when the pilot fails to advise a listening frequency. Then a quandary exists. Should the specialist wait for the pilot's re-call in hopes of catching the frequency light, or "shotgun" on all frequencies, thereby interrupting other communications with other pilots?

The second most common communication error noted by FSS specialists is that of a pilot talking too fast. The pilot is trying to conserve frequency use, but instead creates wasted time and confusion as the specialist unscrambles the message. Conversely, if the specialist talks too fast for comprehension in a noisy cockpit, the pilot is expected to say, "Speak slower."

Pilots filing flight plans while aloft often disrupt the communications flow through an FSS; often these pilots give plan information in haphazard order. FSS specialists suggest you have a flight plan form before you and give information in numbered sequence. Remember to pause between items; the specialist is typing while you're talking.

Many FSS specialists are disappointed with the low number of pilots who volunteer pilot weather reports. Safe traffic flow along the airways is enhanced greatly by these reports. Too often a briefer must tell a preflighting pilot, "No pilot reports received." Call and volunteer a report any time your in-flight weather differs from that given in your preflight briefing. Don't worry about format; the specialist's questions along with your observations will result in a useful pilot report.

Tower Control

Tower jurisdiction normally extends four to five miles from the airport center, upward to 2,500 feet AGL, and the active runway (exceptions to airspace size are noted on sectional charts). Radio contact must be made prior to entry and maintained while within tower's jurisdiction.

Ground control manages surface movement on taxiways designated by yellow centerlines and (optional) yellow shoulder striping. Radio contact with ground control is required before taxiing onto these marked areas.

A few items which bear on common communications errors warrant mention:

1. Unless receiving radar service, make your initial contact 15 miles out. This early contact allows tower time to plan your arrival into the traffic flow. It also gives tower the opportunity to provide you with a pattern approach which best expedites your pattern entry.

2. After entering the traffic area, you must request any unusual maneuvering needed for traffic spacing. Occasionally a pilot makes a downwind 360 on their own volition — to the great excitement of others in the pattern.

3. When departing the pattern, tower expects you to make a standard exit; either straight out or with a 45° turn in the pattern's direction after climbing to pattern altitude. Any non-standard exit must be requested when you advise you are ready for takeoff.

4. Tower normally clears a landing pilot to change to ground control *after* leaving the runway. Many pilots switch frequency while still rolling out. Not only are they taking their eyes off the road in a moving plane, but they

are still under the jurisdiction of tower who may have a last-minute instruction.

5. A taxi clearance for departure clears you to the end of the assigned runway. A request for an intersection takeoff must be stated to, and approved by, ground control.

6. Normally, the ground controller's clearance to an assigned runway allows you to cross inactive runways to get there. A taxi clearance may, however, contain a restriction to "hold short" of a specified runway. In this instance you are required to readback the "hold short" instruction.

7. If you are unfamiliar with the airport, ground control expects you to advise this on initial contact. They will provide "progressive taxi" instructions to runway's end. Pilots who try to find their way on their own often create delays.

8. When in the runup area, remain on ground frequency until you are ready to request takeoff clearance. You are still under the jurisdiction of ground control who may have last-minute instructions.

Approach/Departure Control

When flying within a terminal area and busy with the procedures of arrival or departure, we spot only one-third of our significant traffic. To prevent the collision takes only one pilot to see. But that still leaves a one-third chance. That's where VFR radar service comes in — ATC provides that needed third set of eyes.

Most sizeable airports lie within the watchful range of an approach control. Most rural airfields are in range of an ATC center facility with its frequency easily obtained from FSS.

Initial Arrival Contact

Call early; 30 miles out is usually appropriate. On initial contact, name the facility you're calling, give your full call sign, position, altitude, transponder code, destination, and request radar service. Don't abbreviate your call sign until the controller does so.

Controllers mention two common errors made when pilots report position. First, pilots often mistake distance; confirm with your chart and a landmark. Second, many pilots report their heading, not direction, from the facility.

Penetrating Designated Airspace

If the controller's reply to your initial contact includes your call sign, radio contact has been established and you may enter the designated airspace (Piper 4531 Charlie, standby"). If the controller omits your call sign, you are to remain outside the designated airspace until given clearance (Aircraft calling approach control, standby").

Acknowledgements

If you understand the controller's instructions and you will comply, acknowledge with your call sign. If you don't understand or can't comply, immediately question or advise the controller. To insure traffic separation you are required to confirm changes in altitudes or newly assigned vectors (Piper 31 Charlie leaving 5,000 for 4,000/Piper 31 Charlie turning to 060).

Altitude Assignments

If given an assigned altitude, you cannot leave that altitude unless cleared, either with a new assignment or the phrase, "Resume appropriate VFR altitudes." If not given an assignment, advise the controller of any variations you make to the initially reported altitude.

Vectoring

If not given vectors, you may request the service on a "workload permitting" basis. You may also ask for a vector to clear reported traffic unseen by yourself.

Initial Departure Contact

If you wish radar service on departure, advise ground control on initial contact. After takeoff, tower will advise when you are to contact departure, along with the frequency. Then, just contact the controller with your call sign and you're on your way.

Pilot Responsibilities

Even though under the guidance and instructions of VFR radar service, the pilot is responsible for traffic, terrain and obstacle clearance. You are required to remain VFR — ATC can't see clouds or low visibility — and to comply with all VFR regulations unless cleared to do otherwise.

There is a golden rule to apply when communicating with ATC controllers and FSS specialists: anytime a question arises in your mind, ask it. You will find these professionals happy to oblige with a clearly stated answer. See Figure 13-1.

COMMUNICATIONS LOG

Facility	Station	Station	Station	Station
ATIS	_____	_____	_____	_____
AWOS	_____	_____	_____	_____
FSS	_____	_____	_____	_____
CLNC. DEL.	_____	_____	_____	_____
GND. CON.	_____	_____	_____	_____
TOWER	_____	_____	_____	_____
DEP. CON.	_____	_____	_____	_____
APP. CON.	_____	_____	_____	_____
CENTER	_____	_____	_____	_____
FLT. WTCH.	_____	_____	_____	_____
VOR	_____	_____	_____	_____
NDB	_____	_____	_____	_____
ILS	_____	_____	_____	_____
CTAF	_____	_____	_____	_____
PHONE#	FSS: _____		AWOS: _____	
FSS	_____	_____	_____	_____
AWOS	_____	_____	_____	_____

Figure 13-1
All frequencies and phone numbers can be researched before the flight, either from the sectional or Airport/Facility Directory, then reduced to a communications log for in-flight use.

Chapter 14

Flying in Marginal Visibility

The standards of aviation weather forecasts peg marginal VFR visibility at five miles. This close value, however, may not meet the comfort level of some prudent VFR pilots. Your first line of defense against low visibilities lies in deciding upon a visibility to serve as your own go/no go value. Let personal experience guide you in this decision; schedule a short cross-country through marginal VFR conditions, with a weather-wise instructor aboard. See for yourself what a reported four, five, six mile or more visibility *looks* like, rather than relying on abstract figures of visual range. Then, decide upon your own comfortable minimum visibility for your flying.

Safeguards to Monitor

Once you've pegged the minimum visibility you're content to accept, adopt a number of safeguards to monitor when flying in this marginally acceptable condition.

One, listen very carefully to the weather briefing, and if the low visibility is associated with low clouds or precip, know the cards are starting to stack against you — IFR conditions can lie hidden all around, just beyond your range of flight visibility.

Two, even in dry skies, keep a frequency tuned to Flight Watch. This FAA facility (also called En Route Flight Advisory Service or EFAS) is manned by weather specialists who are also pilots, and can give you up-to-the-minute weather which lies directly ahead and around. All you need to do to receive the information is simply call on their common frequency 122.0 and state your position relative to the nearest VOR. The proper station will respond and can usually contact any plane above three or four thousand AGL.

Third, take extra preflight precautions against getting lost in poor visibility. The greatest hazard that stems from getting lost is the stress it places on the pilot; a stressed pilot sometimes acts in haste, and often makes a wrong decision. Whenever I think of the stress a lost pilot can feel, I think of a particular dual training cross-country I flew with a pilot several years ago. He wasn't a beginner, held a private certificate, had a little over a hundred hours, and was working on his commercial certificate. Part of this training consisted of a three-hour dual flight across unfamiliar ground in far less than ideal VFR conditions. We took off under a 3,000-foot broken base with six miles visibility and the knowledge that afternoon summer rains would meet us en route.

Two hours out, the ceiling turned overcast and dropped quickly to a lead-gray 2,000 feet. The few good landmarks the unpopulated countryside offered began to disappear under the darkening, woolly sky with visibility that continued to lower. The pilot then made a classic error — he deserted his straight heading and started to make shallow turns left and right toward landmarks that did show up. I knew he would soon become lost. I kept my mouth shut but kept close tabs on our changing positions and on the route to the nearby alternate airport I knew we would soon need. A couple of signals confirmed the moment the pilot realized he was lost — his feet began see-sawing the rudder pedals, and he started turning his sectional chart roundabout, hoping the answer would spring from it.

It was then we saw the curtains of rain at the limit of our visibility. The showers were staggered so it looked like we were hemmed in on all sides. The pilot's anxiety grew. I still kept silent and let him get on with his job — and kept my eye on the airport that was now off to our right rear and just inside the veil of rain. Then the overstressed pilot did a most unusual thing. Without really being aware of his actions, I'm sure, he slowly brought the power to near-full throttle and started into a series of left 360s — going nowhere but doing it fast.

Midway through the third circle I tapped him on the shoulder, pointed at his white-knuckled grip on the shoved-in throttle, made circles in the air with a forefinger, and turned an expression toward him that asked "Why?" Then I leaned over, told him I knew exactly where we were, had an airport in sight, and would give him one minute on his own to put a plan together. With the stress diminished, he grinned, picked up his sectional chart, and returned us to the course heading. He quickly figured from his last known position and planted a thumb at our present position on the chart. Then he estimated a heading to the nearest airport symbol, turned the plane and saw the airport. Now he was a pilot who knew where he was, as well as exactly where he was flying to. Every trace of nervousness evaporated and he made a smooth landing despite the gusty crosswind and an approaching heavy line of rain that already had the nearby small town buried under a white froth as we touched down. This talented pilot gave me a very graphic example of how simply getting lost can create stress, which can lead to poor on-the-spot judgement.

Preflight Actions

A few preflight actions are helpful when tackling marginal visibility, and substantially reduce the risk of getting lost. Preplan the simultaneous use of all three navigational methods:

1. Pilotage (use of chart and landmarks),
2. Dead reckoning (use of known winds),
3. Radio (use of VOR).

In planning the flight, take time to draw your course line on your sectional chart. Pencil the line heavily so it won't disappear in a bouncing cockpit. Draw the line even if you're following an airway, for those light blue lines all look alike when things get a bit hectic. Be sure to circle prominent landmarks every 50 or 60 miles, and jot your preflight estimated lapsed time from takeoff that you expect to overfly them. When conditions are marginal, knowing you've flown over an expected landmark at the right time is a tremendous boost to confidence.

Preplan a heading that compensates for the predicted wind. And plan to make use of any VOR radial that establishes a leg of your flight.

Using Full Navigation

Once in the air and flying under marginal visibility, exercise all three methods of navigation simultaneously. Keep a minute-by-minute account of your flight along your penciled line with thumb and landmarks. Pay close attention to your preplanned heading. The most common error that gets pilots lost is the tendency to "wander" when visibility diminishes. Strive also to keep your VOR needle in the "donut" without making "small readjustments" to the bearing selector. Anytime one of the navigational methods seems out of phase with the other two, find out why. If you've been holding a steady heading, for example, and the VOR and landmarks show you drifting off course, look into the reason. It could be that a nearby area of weather has shifted the wind or your heading indicator needs resetting.

Running multiple navigational methods adds another measure of safety to your flight. Low visibility has the ability to take away part of your navigation on a moment's notice. By example, reduced visibility over sparsely landmarked terrain can easily cancel your sectional chart for several minutes at a time. This, however, is no great problem if you continue holding a good heading and VOR needle until the next landmark comes into view. By the same token, poor visibility can force a pilot closer to the ground to maintain visual contact — possibly low enough to eliminate VOR navigation. This should be no great problem for pilots who had been minding their pilotage by dead reckoning.

Defensive Flying

Keep in mind the cold fact that pilots usually see less than half of their significant traffic, even in good visibility. Defensive flying is the answer to avoiding a midair collision in poor visibility. Be concerned with three basic defenses:

1. Increase your "low-visibility" efficiency in spotting aircraft.
2. Make yourself more visible to the other pilots.
3. Avoid unnecessary exposure to congested traffic.

Spotting Traffic

Take the first step toward better plane spotting while you preflight the airplane — clean all the Plexiglas, inside and out. A stuffy load of passengers mixed with the high humidity often associated with poor visibility can give a quick smear of IFR, particularly if the interior surfaces are dirty.

On those flights which tax your vision, put the passengers to work. Give them a preflight briefing and assign each a sector of sky to guard. Most passengers appreciate the responsibility, do a good job, and report traffic with the eagerness of a B-17 tail gunner.

When flying at your personal visibility minimum, take advantage of the service ATC offers: VFR radar traffic advisories. This service is like having an extra set of eyes aboard, but you need to remember that ATC's prime responsibility is to IFR traffic. They can aid VFR pilots on a "time permitting" basis only. If their IFR workload increases, they may stop VFR services without advising you. Nevertheless, any VFR services they do afford serves to increase your efficiency at spotting traffic in marginal visibility.

High Visibility

At the same time, it's just as important to make yourself more visible to other pilots during those flights that are down to your visibility minimums. Take the first steps during your walk-around preflight inspection. Make sure the landing light works and give the strobe a test run. Then, once aloft in the reduced visibility, fly with your landing light blazing away. Even if you do not see head-on traffic (the toughest to spot) it's sure going to notice you! Strobes are very effective during hazy conditions, even in daylight. This cannot be said of the red rotating beacon. During a daylight flight, the plane usually becomes visible before you see the beacon. (If the haze is heavy enough to reflect the winking strobe, however, turn it off. Disorientation can result.)

Another valuable tool in marginal VFR is your transponder. Activate the VFR code (1200) even if you're not in touch with the controller, or flying in airspace that does not require it. At least the controller will know of your presence and alert working traffic to your position.

It's important to increase your own visibility anytime you're approaching an uncontrolled airport; most midairs happen on the final approach to an airport without a control tower. Help other pilots in the pattern spot you by giving frequent position reports on the UNICOM or CTAF frequency. Plan to enter on the downwind leg at a 45° angle; this is where they expect to see you, and the 45° approach gives you a panoramic view of the pattern. If you see a nearby plane and even remotely suspect it does not see you, do two things immediately.

One, announce your position on UNICOM, and two, roll your wings — crisp 30° rolls that attract the attention of even the most unvigilant pilot.

Avoiding Traffic Congestion

When flying in your minimal acceptable visibility, avoid unnecessary exposure to heavy traffic. One way to do this is to choose your cruising altitude defensively. If you intend to fly in excess of 3,000 feet AGL, adhere to the VFR cruising altitude rules of FAR 91.159. These rules have us flying the odd thousand-foot levels plus 500 feet (3,500, 5,500) when on a *magnetic course* (not heading) of 0 through 179°. Even thousand foot levels plus 500 feet (4,500, 6,500) apply when flying a magnetic course of 180 through 359°. This simple system provides a degree of aircraft separation, and enough pilots adhere to the rule to make it an effective deterrent to a midair collision.

These rules, however, do not apply to cruising altitudes *below* 3,000 feet AGL. And conditions causing low visibilities may require you to descend to these lower levels. When flying at these low altitudes, I instruct my students to employ a defensive measure, which you may find useful. Most pilots fly either the 1,000- or 500-foot increments on their altimeters. When flying below 3,000 feet AGL, I ask the students to hang their altimeter needles on the 250 or 750 mark; 2,250 or 2,750 instead of 2,500 or 3,000, for example.

The few planes which have whizzed 250 feet above or below me have proven the practice worthwhile.

Another crowded traffic situation exists at VOR airway intersections. Many pilots navigate to avoid passing directly over these intersections during flight through restricted visibility. Also, it's often wise to avoid an ILS centerline below 3,000 feet AGL within 10 miles of the runway it serves, because you can expect high speed IFR traffic descending through the haze. Rightly or wrongly, the instrument pilot's attention may likely be glued to the panel, and simply not see you.

Finding Your Way

There may come a time in your flying when visibility drops to the point where you find yourself following a highway, river, power line, or railroad. I still like to remember that time as a fledgling commercial pilot, when we flew down to retrieve the hub and bent prop from a medium twin that had tried to land on a southern Florida duster's strip. We took off at mid-morning — Eddie, the veteran, leather-faced maintenance chief, his mechanic, the tool boxes, and I.

We climbed into a hazy summer sky already gathering puff balls of cumulus. The plane was a big, strong cargo hauler that must have been designed by Fruehauf. We had pulled the passenger's seats from the long fuselage. Only the pilot's seat and the small aft bench seat for the mechanics remained, so I had the flight virtually to myself. Midway down the state those puffballs started to build rapidly, and the back of my mind told me the return flight might have complications. But I was still at that point in flying where I thought to show concern was to show a lack of enthusiasm. Besides, I had the controls of a superplane and was being paid to fly it.

We landed at the strip, took an hour in sweltering heat to remove the damaged prop and hoisted it aboard, as distant thunder echoed from a blue-gray massing of cumulus to the north.

Shortly after takeoff, I started detouring weather with wide turns and giving up altitude to stay out of the clouds. What began as scattered white rain squalls quickly gathered into a line of hard weather that kept forcing me westward. Yet common sense and a wind off the Gulf of Mexico told of even heavier weather waiting in that direction.

Respectable turbulence kept the yoke and rudder pedals busy. Constant turns and a sectional chart that kept bouncing off my lap soon had me wondering exactly where we were. The cloud bases had already pushed us below VOR reception, when, over the darkening landmarkless terrain of the state's southern interior, visibility took another plunge. Rain hit the windscreen like a fire hose and sent a bucket of precip roaring across the top of the cockpit. A slight turn pulled us out of the rain again, but I knew things were going to get worse. I had to find an airport fast — but which way? I was flying the bucking airplane two handed and deep into wondering what to do next when I felt the clomp-clomp-clomp of Eddie coming up front for a look. He gripped the seat back, leaned past my right shoulder, and squinted into the grayish white air around us.

"Lost, huh?"

"Uh huh."

"Not to worry — used to live down here... see that road?"

"Uh huh."

"Follow it to the Texaco station... then take a left along the power line to ... be careful! Don't move in too close to the road! ... See! ... See what I mean?"

A southbound Piper Cherokee flew down the road following our landmark at our altitude.

"When you follow roads in this kind of stuff let the other folks fly the center line. Stay as far away as you can, and still see the road. Now follow the power line and turn west on the highway... airport's only another ten minutes. I know the way... we'll make it."

"Uh huh."

And so we picked our way through the ragged scud, Eddie leaning over my shoulder and pointing and guiding with a stubby finger, flickers of lightning reflecting off his age-lined face; me following and flying with uncertain "Uh huhs" all the way to touchdown.

When the visibility is low, let the other folks fly along the road's centerline, sky-wise Eddie advised. In short, that flight was worth

137

the lesson — not to mention the other lessons that came to me from that flight. For instance, about listening to any doubts I had in the back of my mind. Or discovering that my voiced concern does not expel me from the cockpit. And I learned it is foolhardy to leave an airport behind with a suspicious sky ahead without a preflight call to Flight Service. (Even though the field did not have a phone, I'm sure the farmhouse down the road did. Or I could have circled the field to reception altitude and obtained my preflight briefing there.) And to make a 180 back to clear air to sort things out, while there is still plenty of time to do so. Those are early lessons I learned well. Oh, plane and sky still teach me new facts, but nowadays there aren't so many on a single flight. I suppose I'm finally getting it together.

If you asked me to give just three rules-of-thumb for contending with reduced visibility, I'd list:

1. With an instructor on board, see for yourself what different reports of poor visibility actually look like.
2. Decide on a minimum visibility which meets your personal comfort.
3. Take extra time during your preflight preparations to consider how low visibility is going to impact *this* flight, and how you are going to prepare to meet the difficulties. The safety or hazard of any flight is usually determined by the pilot before the wheels even leave the ground.

Chapter 15

Flying Down Under

The FAA describes significant cloud bases less than 3,000 feet AGL as a marginal VFR condition. Your own comfort level for cross-country flying, however, may ask for more. (3,000-foot bases force you to within 2,000 feet AGL if you allow a safe margin of cloud separation.) The best way you can determine your own cloud minimum is to go out and experience low cover — with an instructor on board. Then determine your own comfort level, set your go/no-go cross-country standard accordingly, and stick to it.

Preflight Actions

When clouds are down to your personally-acceptable minimum, take a few extra precautions before you get into the plane. Your main concern is that the clouds may drop below your standard once you are airborne. With this in mind, route your flight to keep alternate airports within 20 minutes flying time of your flight path. In most areas of the country, airports are numerous enough to keep the detouring acceptable. And if the extent of detouring is unacceptable, simply delay the flight until conditions improve. But you can't justify taking off into your marginal weather without giving yourself a series of "outs."

Once your route beneath the clouds is decided, plot the course on the chart with a heavy line. This anticipates a strong reliance on pilotage should clouds push you below VOR reception range. To further aid pilotage, circle prominent landmarks at 20- to 30-minute intervals along the route and jot down next to them the estimated lapsed time from departure. This lets you better monitor your progress and gives a number of intermediate goals as you fly through marginal conditions. Choose landmarks that will stand out even from the perspective of low-altitude flying. This means the landmarks should be large or tall — for example, towns, bodies of water, airports, or strobed TV antennas. Roads, streams, or railways are hard to spot when the going gets low. As a hedge against clouds lowering further, circle any ridge or obstacle that rises within 1,500 feet of your expected cruise altitude.

A hazard pilots must face when traveling beneath relatively low clouds is the military low-altitude training routes (marked on your sectional). These military routes normally lead to restricted areas, and jets fly these corridors in excess of 300 knots within 1,500 feet of the ground. The big problem is, you often can't see the jets soon enough to dodge them. If you anticipate having to cruise within 2,000 feet AGL and your route lies within 50 miles of a restricted area, consult with FSS to see if the training routes serving the area are active. If the restricted area and its routes *are* active, you'd be wise to detour your low flying elsewhere. (A few years ago, I flew wildlife survey flights near restricted areas served by low-altitude training routes; discussed in Chapter 11. After a few close whooshes, I traveled to the military base to talk to a flying officer who was involved in the flights. I told him of my inability to see his plane in a timely fashion and waited for a suggestion. He told me we were even — the fighter pilots can't see the small planes either.)

When the clouds are down to your acceptable minimum and you receive your briefing from FSS, pay extra attention to three factors:

1. Are the clouds expected to get lower? If so, stick to your acceptable preflight minimums.

2. Is there a second marginal condition waiting for you — reduced visibility, rain, turbulence? If so, think twice about going.

3. Is your arrival time near sunset? If so, consider an early darkness under the low clouds that may get lower suddenly with the cooling air.

In-flight Considerations

Once aloft under your minimum acceptable cloud bases, recognize that low clouds place you and your plane at a disadvantage. This calls for a 100% effort on your part. Minimize the distractions of conversation and sight-seeing. You have a full-time job at hand — delivering plane and passengers safely to the destination airport.

It takes concentration and hard work to keep a minute-to-minute track of your present position when flying under low clouds. It means keeping a thumb along your course line as landmarks drift by while you're equally busy flying the plane accurately, managing communications, evaluating the surrounding weather, constantly updating your alternate courses of action, and looking out for traffic in the limited airspace beneath the clouds. But you must keep track of your exact position. The moment you become uncertain of where you are, things tend to go wrong and those clouds always seem to pick that time to come down lower. And racing clouds to the ground is no fun if you don't know which way it is to the finish line.

As you fly cross-country under low cloud cover, maintain a weather watch with FSS or Flight Watch. It's certainly reasonable to call at 20-minute intervals to update any weather changes ahead and behind and at your destination and alternate airports.

Alternate airports are your best insurance when flying in your minimum acceptable weather. In addition to having an alternate in mind, be sure to mentally update the estimated heading and time to it every few minutes. Wherever possible, use paved airports as your alternates; sod fields are difficult to find when you fly lower than normal. If the clouds force you to within 2,000 feet of the ground, turn toward your nearest alternate at that time and tell FSS of your plan. Any further cloud lowering could put you in a serious position.

Over the Top

When preplanning a VFR cross-country flight, the question often arises: "Should I plan to fly beneath the cloud layer or go VFR over the top?" It's often safer to fly beneath the cover. This assumes, of course, the bases meet your personal weather minimum for safe flight. If your minimum for safe travel is not met, you are better advised to delay or postpone rather than go VFR-On-Top.

If you decide you must plan the flight above the clouds, you — along with a FSS briefer — must carefully weigh the risk. First, are the reported clouds no greater than "scattered" with no second layer above them? VFR above broken or overcast is out of the question. Will the bases permit safe VFR beneath? Then, does the forecast indicate either an improvement or no change, and are the destination and alternate airports expected to be no lower than your personal minimum, an hour before to an hour after the expected time of arrival? Finally, you'd be wise to get a *current* pilot report. It's likely that FSS is in communication with a plane on the proposed route, and if requested, the FSS briefer can contact that pilot for a report.

Once in the air, you must reevaluate the decision to climb above the clouds. While still beneath, determine the extent of coverage and look for a second, higher layer. Unless those clouds are widely scattered (less than a quarter of the sky covered) with no additional clouds above, you're better advised to stay beneath. It's often difficult to estimate cloud coverage from beneath. The slant-view hides the size of the open areas. But a look downward toward the cloud shadows on the ground tells the story.

Before climbing over the clouds, take a final look ahead for any darkening that foretells of significant clouds a little farther along the route.

From the moment you level off above the widely scattered clouds, stay in touch with the nearest FSS and keep in tune with any changes in the weather around you. It's often difficult to visually determine any closing of the cloud cover that lies ahead. The slanted perspective at only 1,000 or 2,000 feet above the clouds is the problem. You must stay alert for buildups that spell increased coverage ahead and keep close tabs on the clouds immediately beneath the plane.

Any thickening of the cloud cover is reason for an immediate retreat and descent. No VFR pilot should continue above closing scattered clouds hoping for an improvement "just ahead." Any hesitation could find plane and pilot trapped. I've seen widely scattered clouds become overcast in less than a minute of travel. It can happen more quickly than the time it takes to get the plane down through a clear area in the gathering cover.

Should you find yourself caught above the clouds — through miscalculation, flawed information, or other reason — take three immediate steps to prepare an escape. First, mark your position and time on your sectional chart as your last landmarks disappear. This helps you keep a running estimate of position as you later tick off attained positions along the course line at ten-minute intervals. (A common mistake is a failure to maintain the course. It's tempting to turn the plane as you search for a way down. It's far better, however, to hold the plane steady and let your head do the swiveling.)

Second, you should throttle back to conserve fuel. A ceiling can cover an extensive area and remain there for a considerable time.

And third, you should quickly alert FSS of your predicament. Together with FSS, a decision can be made as to the best direction to fly. Don't hesitate to work through the dilemma with a ground facility. A satisfactory answer to this situation can rarely be reached on your own. FSS *wants* to help and that's what they're there for. You would then be wise to contact ATC for vectors to the VFR letdown point for an escape before encountering instrument conditions.

Caught Above

The pilot caught above the clouds faces three common sources of unavoidable instrument conditions.

1. The clouds may extend beyond the plane's remaining range.
2. The plane may become trapped between converging layers.
3. Building clouds may out-climb the airplane.

Picture yourself riding as a passenger in the plane, VFR on top. FSS advises your pilot that the nearest reported VFR lies 100 miles from your position. They also advise of strong headwinds from that direction — and the fuel gauges are already between the half and quarter marks. Or picture the plane between layers. With ground and horizon lost and those layers converging, vertigo is likely — with loss of control then an almost certainty. Or finally, picture the clouds building upward. Your pilot climbs to stay in the clear, but it's easy to see the clouds are rapidly outclimbing the plane — with the plane already nearing its service ceiling.

Whatever the source, the IFR specter usually gives the pilot several minutes to comprehend the inevitable loss of VFR references. And it's at this point we leave our pilot, gathering thoughts for the decisions and actions to come. Because the uncertain and unproven procedures for extracting a VFR pilot from

IFR conditions are beyond the scope of our conversation here; they're a subject in themselves.

Personal Responsibility and Commitment

Crowding the clouds closer than your experience, extent of planning, or pilot capability safely allows is neither adventuresome nor stout-hearted; it's foolhardy, scary, and irresponsible to yourself, your family aground, passengers on board, and to your fellow pilots. When coping with marginal cloud conditions, commit yourself to a three-pronged defense. First, through personal observation and experience (with an instructor on board) decide for yourself your own go/no go cloud criteria for safe flight. And once decided upon, stick to your guns. Don't let any outside pressures for action push you beyond your own common sense.

Second, give extra effort toward flight planning. Listen with great detail to your weather briefing. Then take the time necessary to visualize when and where you're going to encounter the condition and picture the plans and actions you intend to use to keep the hazards at bay and to provide yourself a series of "outs." To do otherwise is to simply rely on chance. And the very nature of chance is that it must someday turn against us.

Finally, if cross-country flying is a part of your life aloft, commit yourself to the ultimate defense. Decide *now* that you'll begin training for your instrument pilot rating — the ultimate defense against less-than-ideal flying weather. Know that your passengers aboard and family aground will silently thank you for going the extra mile that brings further safety and excellence to your cockpit.

Part IV

Arrival

The beacon ahead — the coast — the harbor with two breakwater arms stretched out to the sea — terribly rough sea, even in the harbor. We have never landed on pontoons at night.

Anne Morrow Lindbergh, *Locked Rooms and Open Doors*

Chapter 16

Bullseye Landings

Old pros almost always make those seemingly effortless landings that touch down right on target. Believe me, it's an illusion; each landing isn't "effortless." Those old pros create the illusion through the simple expedient of working very hard to make each and every landing an accuracy landing. Soon, that repeated, intense effort becomes trained reflex. But the work is still there; it only *looks* easy. This illusion of effortless accuracy is available to any pilot willing to deliver the old pro's simple formula — make every landing an accuracy landing.

As a precision maneuver, an accuracy landing plants your tires on the runway at a point within 200 feet beyond your intended touchdown target. It's not hard to do if you follow a few tips.

A Precise Pattern

First, fly a precise traffic pattern. Keep your downwind leg a half-mile from the runway, at pattern altitude, and a pattern speed of 1.7 x power-off, flaps-up stall. A downwind leg a half-mile from the runway is close enough to prevent delaying other traffic, yet gives adequate time to plan your approach. A common error when landing at small airports is to scale down the pattern. This rushes planning. Fly the same pattern you use at Bigtown Municipal. Keep your downwind leg parallel to the runway: define the downwind leg's ground track by selecting landmarks to help *visualize* (very important) the parallel flight path. Then watch for any wind drift against your visualized line and immediately correct for it.

A pattern altitude of 900 feet AGL is suitable for most light aircraft, but abide by any established pattern altitude at your field. Allow yourself only a 40-foot margin for error so you may begin every approach to an accuracy landing from the same height.

A pattern speed of 1.7 x stall works well in most single-engine lightplanes. This is slow enough to allow adequate planning time, yet fast enough to prevent undue delays to the traffic flow. And it's close enough to approach speed that a transition to that speed is made easier.

Planning the Touchdown Bullseye

Begin the approach to your accuracy landing from the downwind leg, abeam your intended touchdown target. It's very important to have a specific, highly visible target. Select the second centerline stripe beyond the numbers as your touchdown target — with its midpoint as the bullseye. Centerline stripes are normally a standard 120 feet in length, separated by 80 feet. Thus, if you touch down before the midpoint of the succeeding stripe, you are within the desired 200 feet of the bullseye. Choosing the second stripe as your target allows a safe margin for error in case of an undershoot; don't use the runway numbers as your touchdown target. (Frankly, pilots who turn to me in the cockpit and announce, "I'm gonna plant it on the numbers" start me squirming in the seat.)

Flying the Approach

At the abeam position, reduce power to 1700 RPM or 17" MP (or as appropriate to the plane you fly) and trim to the exact, specific approach speed recommended by your airplane's flight manual. This power setting permits a manageable descent in most light singles so only minor adjustments during the letdown are needed. A partial-power descent holds three advantages over power-off approach:

1. Your engine responds quicker to a power increase that might be needed to correct for a low glide path.
2. You have greater flexibility. With partial power, you can either increase or decrease throttle. On a power-off approach, you can only increase it.
3. A power-off approach causes an excessive sink rate that's often difficult to manage with accuracy; partial power keeps sink in hand.

If you slow to approach speed early enough in the approach, you'll avoid unnecessary trouble. Otherwise, the activities of the approach may come at you faster than you can sort them out. Slow to approach speed before you turn base leg, and the approach will unfold before you in seemingly slow motion.

Plan the approach to your accuracy landing with partial flaps rather than full flaps (check you plane's manual for precautions). This gives your landing descent greater flexibility. If, for example, you see on final that you are overshooting, you still have additional flaps in reserve with which to shorten the approach. On the other hand, if you are undershooting, you will need a smaller power increase than would have been required with flaps fully extended. Large power changes on final can drastically affect an approach and make for a poor landing.

An approach flown with partial flaps offers advantages over one flown with flaps up. With flaps already partially extended, the glide path immediately steepens with the application of additional flaps. However, the airplane's response to flaps is not as rapid if your flaps are extended from the completely retracted position. Flaps also increase the margin between the flight manual's approach speed and stalling speed. Also, the resulting lower nose adds to straight-ahead visibility during round out and touchdown.

Turning to Final

On base leg, plan your turn to final at an altitude that helps assure an accurate touchdown. You can easily do this if you pick a landmark on final, one-half mile out from your touchdown target and let that landmark serve as your final approach fix. Here's how it works:

Reduce your power and retrim on the downwind leg, opposite your touchdown target, at 900 feet AGL (assuming this is an acceptable pattern altitude for your airport). Now your goal is to gauge your descent so you cross your final-fix landmark: at 400 feet AGL. After you turn base leg (you're now about 700 feet AGL), eyeball the distance remaining to the landmark against the altitude you've yet to lose in order to cross your final fix at 400 feet AGL. If you think you're too low, add 50 RPM. If too high, reduce throttle by 50 RPM. Then reevaluate your *altitude to lose* versus *distance to travel*, at each 50 feet of altitude lost. Make power changes by 50 RPM increments accordingly, as you descend to your final-fix altitude. The point is this — the half-mile reference point gives you a visible intermediate altitude objective. Without this it's very difficult to manage your descent throughout the entire approach which involves two changes of direction. And by reevaluating your glide path *throughout* the approach, you eliminate the need for any desperate bid with power on short final that virtually eliminates any chance at a smooth landing.

Final Approach

Look for traffic, turn final just outside your final fix, and lock your eyes on the touchdown target. Cross the fix at 400 feet AGL, and look for the *apparent motion* of the target. The apparent-motion method almost guarantees a touchdown on target: If your target appears to move upward or away, your glide path will land you short. If the target appears to move downward or toward you, you'll land long. A target that appears motionless has you landing very near to the mark. (Actually, you land slightly beyond the target as your glide path flattens out a little closer to the ground. For a perfect bullseye, allow for this slight overshoot.)

From the final approach fix to touchdown, change your power in small 50 RPM increments to hold your target motionless. Power changes much greater than 50 RPM drastically alter your glide path and make an accurate touchdown unlikely. Retrim with each small power change or flap adjustment, as accurate airspeed control is virtually impossible without doing so. And a consistent, accurate airspeed (within 3 knots) is critical to accurate touchdowns. By example, each 5-knot excess increases your landing distance about 12% in a typical light aircraft.

Every Landing an Accuracy Landing

Once you're satisfied with your accuracy landing, use your technique to conclude every flight. You may occasionally miss your target; however, your efforts toward accuracy will reward you with a smooth landing — far smoother than an approach to land "somewhere in the first third of the runway." It's the difference between a half-hearted effort and a 100% effort — and that's *all* the difference. Then, very soon, you'll discover your conscious effort has become trained reflex. You'll deliver those "seemingly effortless" landings time after time after time.

Chapter 17

Short-Field Cunning

Plan your approach to the short runway with all the caution and cunning of a pro quarterback committed to a fourth-down pass from his own end zone. In addition, keep in mind two reasons that short fields have produced more than their fair share of accidents: most of today's pilots received their training on long, paved, well maintained runways, and most of today's airplanes are designed to operate from those runways. Armed with these two facts, you can develop a method that provides fail-safe measures to stop the action when a hazardous situation arises. Your procedure should provide a series of "outs" for the inexperienced short-field pilot or the plane that's ill equipped for short-field landings.

Preflight Planning

Begin your defensive short-field technique by following a golden rule of thumb: research your airplane's landing performance chart and your destination's expected runway conditions before you depart — not as you arrive at that airport. Not only is this good procedure, but Federal Aviation Regulations mandate it: FAR 91.103 *Preflight Action* reads in part: "Each pilot in command shall, before beginning a flight, become familiar with all available information concerning that flight. That information must include ... runway lengths of intended use... aircraft flight manual takeoff and landing distance data... aircraft performance under expected values of airport elevation and runway slope, aircraft weight, and wind and temperature."

Your preflight weather briefing can disclose the destination's surface wind and temperature expected at your estimated time of arrival. Runway surface and length, field elevation, and runway heading (to estimate anticipated headwind and crosswind components) can be found in the *Airport/Facility Directory*.

Pilots flying to an unfamiliar short field — especially those marked with an R on the sectional chart — should anticipate possible adverse runway conditions. A briefing from a pilot who knows the field or a long-distance call to the field itself may give you invaluable information.

Preflight Fail-Safe Measures

Employ a preflight fail-safe measure designed to prevent a possible hazardous arrival even before the action starts — allow an adequate margin for safety. Aircraft landing charts usually express required distance in two forms: ground roll and total-to-clear-obstacles. Ground roll is the distance it takes to bring the plane to a stop once it touches down. The total-to-clear-obstacle distance contemplates an approach over a standard 50-foot obstacle near the approach end of the runway. This distance provides the approximate total needed to descend over a 50-foot obstacle to a touchdown point and bring the plane to a stop. In reality, this is very nearly the glide path we fly even when no obstacle exists. So it is this figure — total-to-clear-obstacle — that is of paramount value to the pilot considering the safety of the landing. And to this figure you must add a fail-safe margin of safety. Unless you're very good, don't plan a landing unless the runway length provides at least 150% of the total-to-clear-obstacle distance for the landing conditions you expect will prevail at your time of arrival.

This safety margin is necessary in order to prevent an unexpected overrun caused by a situation beyond the pilot's control, such as a wet patch of grass, a down grade near runway's end, or a headwind that suddenly dies. Consider landing a fully loaded Skyhawk at a sea-level grass field on a hot windless afternoon, for example. The landing chart calls for 1,600 feet total-to-clear-obstacle distance. Unless that runway exceeds 2,400 feet (1600 x 1.5) or unless you're an ace, don't try it.

Remember, real obstacles don't always come in standard 50-foot heights. When calculating the landing distance over higher obstacles, add the air travel distance of the approach for each additional 50 feet of obstacle height. (Air travel distance equals the stated total-to-clear-obstacle distance, minus ground roll.)

Short-Field Procedure and Pilot Technique

Begin your short-field procedure with a slow overfly of the strip, 500 feet above pattern altitude. Look hard for company, then study the runway surface. Note activities on the field, such as gliders, mowers, or maybe even cows, and estimate your headwind component from the wind sock. (Socks stiffen at 15 knots; a 45° droop indicates 7 or 8 knots.) While still above the airport, pick two marks on the runway that will ensure accuracy and safety — your touchdown target and your go-around point.

In-flight Fail-Safe Measures

You must keep a definite touchdown target in sight during final approach to prevent undershooting or overshooting the landing. Choose a mark about a quarter to a third of the way down the runway. This is far enough to prevent a misjudgment that might cause you to land short or clip a fence, yet it's near enough to the threshold to conserve adequate runway for touchdown and rollout. On sod or turf strips, that worn patch where the local pilots touch makes a good bullseye. Without a visible touchdown target, you may not recognize a poor glidepath until you're nearly down, and your last-second bid with power or flaps is bound to produce an uncontrolled and unsafe landing.

It's just as important to choose a visible go-around point. A definite landmark, at which you must execute a timely go-around, is your only guarantee that adequate braking distance will remain after the wheels touch down.

Your go-around point should be an easily recognizable landmark halfway down the runway. If overall runway length exceeds 150% of the required total-to-clear-obstacle distance, half the runway length will normally provide safe stopping distance. On unpaved runways, a convenient midpoint mark on the runway usually doesn't exist. More often than not, you must be satisfied with a landmark alongside the runway (parked plane, wind sock, bush or building). However, you do need some visible go-around point. While overflying the airport, decide to automatically execute a go-around if your tires haven't touched down by the time your go-around point zips by.

When dealing with a short runway, you cannot leave that critical decision to those last few, tense seconds as you skim along its rapidly diminishing length. If you do delay your decision, you may likely find yourself mentally committed to a landing, regardless of the hazard. I'm convinced that most landing accidents would have been avoided, had the pilot just made a timely go-around, and tried again. Accordingly, I advise my students: plan your first decision as a go-around. Then, if everything is still OK as your touchdown target arrives, put you secondary decision into play — land the airplane.

Approaching the Pattern

After you've made an overhead scan of the runway, turn to a landmark two or three miles away that will let you enter the downwind leg at a 45° angle. Descend to pattern altitude as you fly outbound, and once again scout the area for traffic as you fly back toward the airport. Remind yourself of two facts. Most midairs occur during approaches to uncontrolled airports, and all runways are active and available for use at these airports — not just the one favored by the wind. Throughout your approach, watch for planes approaching or departing any runway — including the opposite end of the one you intend to use.

As you approach the downwind leg, mentally trace and visualize with landmarks the track you want your pattern to follow. Beware though, many pilots erroneously scale down the size of their pattern when approaching a short field. This usually produces a time-shortened approach that ends with a high, fast final leg. Trace out the same pattern you use at Bigtown Municipal.

Downwind Leg

Turn downwind and set your throttle back to approach speed early in the pattern. Be sure to retrim with each power reduction, and have the airplane at approach speed before you turn base leg. This slows the action and helps a pilot's thinking stay ahead of the airplane.

While flying the downwind leg, pick the remaining landmark you need for your short-field procedure: your final-approach fix. Choose a landmark on final that lies a half-mile from your touchdown target. To quickly estimate a half-mile final-fix point, just compare the distance to the known runway length. If the runway is 2,000 to 3,000 feet long, for example, the half-mile landmark lies about one runway length out.

Plan to cross your half-mile final-fix point at 400 feet AGL. This ensures a fairly accurate glide path that's neither embarrassingly high nor dangerously low, and only small power adjustments should be necessary to correct for any variations in normal headwinds. In this way, you eliminate the need for a power-off, ton-of-bricks descent, or a high-power, paint-it-on-the-carrier-deck approach.

Base Leg

When you turn to base, review the two procedures you must mobilize to execute a short-field landing:

1. Slightly steepen your approach path once any obstacles are behind you. This produces a short final that consumes the least amount of runway length in air travel. Start a smooth, steady power reduction as you pass over the obstacle. A perfect rate of throttle reduction will achieve zero thrust just as the tires touch.
2. Touch down at the slowest safe ground speed to produce the shortest safe ground roll.

While still on base leg then, lower half the flaps you intend to use and retrim with each flap increment. Airspeed is easier to control in a properly trimmed airplane; distractions do not easily result in an unexpected nose-up or nose-down attitude during your approach. Set your throttle at 1500 to 1700 RPM and fly a shallow turn which puts you on final slightly outside your final-fix landmark. Continue to evaluate your rate of descent on base with each 50-foot decrease on the altimeter as you close the distance to that landmark, then use small throttle movements to cross the fix at 400 feet AGL.

Final Leg

Turn final, extend full flaps as you cross the final-fix landmark, and trim the plane to it's slowest recommended approach speed. Then shift your attention to the touchdown target and use small power variations to maintain an accurate descent. Use this time-tested visual reference: if your touchdown target appears to move downward or toward you, the glide path is too high; you're overshooting. Conversely, if the target appears to move upward or away from you, you're undershooting. But if the point appears motionless, you'll touch down very nearly on target.

If obstacle clearance is a factor, use another visual reference to assure clearance. After you establish your glide path, look at your touchdown target and then at the tip of the obstacle lying between you and that target. As long as the apparent vertical distance between the obstacle tip and the target increases, you should clear the obstacle. If, however, that gap diminishes, you may not have clearance (see Figure 17-1).

Keep your mind ready for a possible go-around from the moment you start descending over your half-mile final-fix. Several occurrences can make a pull-up advisable. An uncorrected crosswind certainly merits a go-around, as do pedestrians or vehicles on the runway, or a taxiing airplane that arouses suspicion. You'd be wise to add power and go around any time a large power change or flap application is needed to correct a glidepath error. A desperate bid with flaps or throttle on short final spoils even the expert's landing, and may lead to a damaged airplane. Without question, pull up if your wheels aren't on the ground by the time

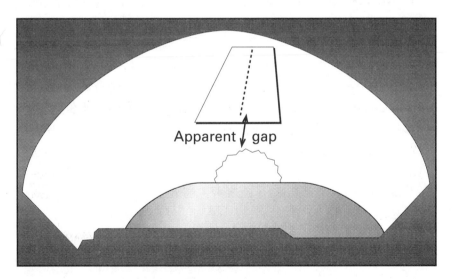

Figure 17-1
The increasing or diminishing apparent gap between the tip of the obstacle and your touchdown target offers a visual aid with which to assure obstacle clearance.

your go-around point whizzes by. Stay mentally prepared for a go-around as you descend to the runway.

In fact, when landing at an unfamiliar short field, I plan my first approach to the runway as a go-around. I believe a deliberate go-around lends three safety factors to my short-field procedure. First, it gives me a practice shot at a landing technique I don't often have a chance to use, since most of my flying is from long paved runways. A preplanned go-around also makes the idea of an emergency pull-up on the second pass mentally acceptable. Many pilots come to regret a short-field just because they hesitated to make the go-around their logic told them they needed. Vanity, fixation, mental inflexibility — whatever the reason for ignoring logic, the results are the same. Finally, a deliberate go-around from the first approach lets me take a close look at what may be a questionable runway surface. Debris, rough area and soft spots are more easily spotted on a low, slow pass than from pattern altitude. For these reasons, I feel an intentional go-around is worth the time and effort. Just be sure to tell your passengers what you have in mind.

After Touchdown

After you touch down on a short runway, hold the yoke full aft, apply firm, steady braking without locking the wheels, and leave the flaps extended for aerodynamic braking. Keep your eyes straight ahead; short runways are usually on the narrow side. If you look inside for a flap handle, carburetor heat knob, or any other distraction, you may swerve. If the runway is unpaved, hold full-aft stick during roll-out and taxi to help smooth out the ride.

There's one final fail-safe measure you should consider. If your destination is indeed short and you lack experience, an hour of short-field procedure — dual with an instructor — might be a good investment. Then you'll be prepared to fully enjoy the challenge of short-field landings.

Chapter 18

The Lost Art of Flying

When grizzled old pilots sit in the lobby of a modern airport, they tend to hunch in the far corner of the room and grumble about how the slip to a landing has become "the lost art of flying." And of course they're right. After all, what good is a slip nowadays? In the old days it was the pilot's only means to steepen an approach over the treetops and onto the short landing strip. But now we have efficient flaps and longer runways. Therefore, the slip to a landing became an outmoded, inefficient, and unsophisticated means to steepen an approach. But it also provides some of the greatest fun flying has to offer.

Pilots who can skillfully slip their airplanes seem to get no end of pleasure from the procedure — stiffening the slip to increase the rate of sink, reducing the sink at will with a deft flick of aileron and rudder, steepening the glidepath a final time with a mash of rudder, landing the airplane exactly where they wish. The difference between an accuracy landing and "just getting it down" is whether or not the upwind wheel plants exactly dead center on a hubcap-size touchdown target.

Probably the first step in learning the slip is to simply stand near a runway's end and watch a bunch of planes slip in over the tree line, studying the maneuver from a vantage point outside the cockpit. You won't find these slips going on at a big city airport catering to Bonanzas, Mooneys, King Airs and the like. Instead, go out to the uncontrolled sod field that fills its Saturday pattern with Luscombes, Cubs, and Taylorcrafts. Study each little ship as the pilots slip to a butterfly touchdown on the turf. And, make no mistake, those pilots don't really need to slip. They could easily make two or three landings on the average country runway of today. They do a slip just because it's fun and looks good.

Why Slip?

The purpose of a slip to a landing is merely to steepen the glidepath on final approach without increasing the airplane's airspeed. Pilots accomplish this feat by simply flying the airplane sideways through the air.

To see how this maneuver works, imagine a pilot who has just turned from base leg and now is established on final approach. At this point, the pilot realizes the approach is too high and decides to steepen it with a slip.

The first move is simple: close the throttle to idle power. It would make little sense to lose altitude with a slip while maintaining power that tends to reduce the rate of sink.

Crosswind Down the Approach

Once the throttle is closed, the next step is to remind yourself which way the crosswind is blowing over the runway. True, the direction of the crosswind has little effect on the slip during the final approach. But somewhere prior to touchdown, you must shift from the "slip to a landing" to the "slip for crosswind correction." And this shift is easier to accomplish if you've slipped with the "down-wing" into the wind.

Assuming you're facing a left crosswind, you'd establish the slip by using considerable aileron to bank left while simultaneously mashing in firm right rudder to swing the airplane's fuselage to the right and at an angle to the forward flight path.

With equal firm aileron and rudder pressures, the airplane descends straight ahead but flies sidewise through the air — banked left, yawed right.

Controlling Sink Rate

It's this sidewise flight attitude that steepens the approach. The attitude presents the side of the fuselage to the oncoming relative wind. The excess drag that the maneuver creates causes the airplane's descent to steepen appreciably. And yet the steepness of the approach is easy to control. If you wish to steepen the approach even further, apply additional aileron and rudder pressure. The extra rudder swings even more fuselage into the wind, while extra aileron keeps the descent going straight ahead.

Conversely, if you wish to lessen the airplane's sink rate, just decrease control pressures. This reduces the fuselage's sidewise attitude and lessens drag. You can then control the rate of descent to make a perfect glide path toward the touchdown target.

Managing Airspeed

But here's the tricky part: for a touchdown right on the mark, you must maintain proper approach speed throughout the slip to the landing. And doing that means knowing your airplane, since in many airplanes the airspeed indicator is inaccurate during a slip. This inaccuracy stems from a pitot tube which is not aligned with the wind, and a static port that may no longer be receiving neutral pressure as the fuselage is turned into the wind. Add to this the fact that the airspeed changes during the cross-controlled attitude. Many airplanes slow down in the slip, and you must lower the nose slightly to maintain approach speed.

Some airplanes, on the other hand, may tend to gain speed. In either case, you must know your airplane well enough to determine the correct airspeed by the sound of the wind over the windscreen and feel of the controls. As you roll out of your slip at the bottom end of the approach, the airplane's nose must be returned quickly to the attitude that will continue to produce the correct approach speed.

Once you've brought your plane down accurately toward the touchdown target, you make a shift from the "slip to a landing" to the "crosswind correction slip." To do this, simply release enough rudder pressure to let the fuselage align with the flight path and the runway center line, maintaining just enough aileron to correct for the crosswind touchdown and roll out.

Different Slips

Pilots sometimes ask, "what is the difference between a slip used to correct for a crosswind and a slip used to lose altitude?" The only difference lies in the degree of the slip, the degree of control pressure. In a slip used to correct for a crosswind, only enough aileron is used to prevent the plane from drifting, and only enough rudder is applied to keep the fuselage aligned with the centerline. In correcting for a left crosswind, for example, the airplane is banked to the left, but the nose points straight ahead. In a slip used to lose altitude, however, stronger rudder pressure is applied to deflect the fuselage away from the flightpath, while matching opposite aileron keeps the airplane's flightpath on course. The airplane's wings are banked left while the plane's nose is pointed right, for example. Think of the differences in control use in this way:

Slip to a landing

Ailerons — used to maintain flightpath.
Rudder — used to deflect fuselage.

Crosswind correction slip

Ailerons — used to prevent drift left or right of center line.
Rudder — used to keep fuselage in center line alignment

Practice at Altitude

Those scant moments on final approach don't allow adequate time in which to perfect your slip to a landing. Rather, begin your in-flight practice by taking your airplane to 3,000 feet AGL (after reviewing your airplane's flight manual to make certain prolonged slips are an approved maneuver; a few models prohibit them). At this altitude, align your airplane with a long, straight road and throttle back, leaving 1500 RPM in the engine to keep it warm. Then practice rolling into and out of the slip as you descend several hundred feet.

Preserving the Lost Art

After you feel comfortable with the cross-control attitude of the slip to a landing, carry your practice to a runway for the full approach and landing sequence. Practice until you're good — really good. Then carry your act to an audience that will appreciate your skill — a country airport pattern. Spend an afternoon in the company of those Cubs, Luscombes, and Taylorcrafts as you help preserve "the lost art of flying."

Chapter 19

Family Values and Tailwheels

Some years ago a beautiful white-with-green-trim Cessna 120 from the 1940's became a part of my life. The saucy little two-seat tailwheeler was still equipped as it had been when first rolled from the company's works three decades before. No NAVAIDs and no gyros, not even a radio.

But there was nowhere we wished to go that we couldn't; few places we didn't. Navigation was a snap: chart, wind across the treetops, E6B and a Timex that never failed. A bobbling Airguide compass, angles eyeballed off section lines, and a remembrance of childhood geography classes finished out the system. The simple plane was a basic product of simpler times that held less intense expectations. We two were in constant, personal touch with our country rolling out just a half-mile beneath us.

Part fabric, part metal, the little ship was a child of the earlier decade's Cessna Airmaster. In turn, the small 120 became parent to the next generation's Skyhawks and Skylanes, who themselves carried the values and traditions forth, giving birth to later, sleeker ships that ran faster, climbed higher, and ranged farther.

As of late, I've been mulling this over in my mind — this lineage. People are a lot like airplanes: grandparents, parents, children. Grandparents there to show the children from whence they came and to serve as gentle reminders of time-tested, unchanging values that bind generation to generation: tradition.

Parents to help them envision what they may become; providing the tools with which to make it possible.

And the children. Belonging neither to parents nor community but only to themselves; wishing most of all — often with youthfully inarticulate words and actions — to simply please their parents. Then, to become in their own time able to run faster, climb higher, range farther: lineage.

As pilots we've been given the opportunity to best serve the children around us. As pilots we live out a portion of our lives aloft where only truths and correct actions prevail. As pilots we live a life of values learned, instilled, and put into play. Plane and sky tell us there are values at altitude worthy of passing forward. As pilots we're given the unique opportunity to let the "ripple effect" of our flying say to young dreamers: one day you too may learn of the values discovered in a perfectly executed takeoff, or a perfectly held altitude and heading, or perfectly flown approach that touches down right on the mark. But, until that day, trust the dictates of your own logic. Listen to those who have traveled before you —but not too rigidly. For whether they're 50 or 60 or 75, none have yet gained one-tenth of what you dream of achieving before the next decade is out. And if your logic tells you what is commonly called right is wrong, hold faith with your own reason. Let your life accept the pleasures of your *own* authority — and the responsibilities for your *own* mistakes. Use each win, each loss, as a stepping stone toward your own total awareness of who you are and what you expect from yourself. And in that regard your life will be a lot like flying.

As parents and grandparents we're both fortunate and privileged to pass forward the values and traditions of the cockpit where only truth, correct action, and personal responsibility prevail. Maybe in actions rather than words, for actions rightly taken rarely need explaining, even to a child.

Airmaster, 120, Skyhawk, Citation: lineage. Airplanes are a lot like people.

Tailwheel State of Mind

I'm not sure just why I've always enjoyed teaching tricycle-gear pilots how to fly tailwheel airplanes. I don't really think a tailwheel teaches a pilot better landings. I've seen tailwheel-trained pilots wobble their planes all over the ground. I've seen tricycle-trained pilots handle their planes with absolute precision. Pilots who decide on excellence will deliver that quality no matter what kind of plane they fly; excellence is a matter of pilot, not plane.

Why then, do I enjoy watching pilots master those little puppies? I think it just has to do with a state of mind. No matter how long you've been at flying, there's something about a tailwheeler that recalls the legacy; magnificent pilots in flying machines, canvas-armored Sopwiths, barnstormers, the night mail and now you, seeking a physical contact with aviation's golden age of flying.

Let me say this right off — landing a tailwheeler is no more difficult than landing a nosewheeler. It's just different, that's all. But let me also say the difference is great enough you can't expect to teach yourself tailwheel landings. A good flight instructor is called for. An incident I witnessed a few years ago points out this need.

Dual Instruction

I'd just landed at a neighboring airport and taxied past the FBO to the maintenance hangar. The field had once served the Navy and the hangar was one of those cavernous metal buildings with mammoth doors that could swallow two blimps.

It was a slow, summer day and several mechanics and line crew stood talking just inside the hangar, taking advantage of the cooling breeze and protecting shade. Outside, across the sunny concrete ramp, the new owner of an old tailwheeler was polishing the windscreen. The pretty little pre-war Luscombe stood high on stiff legs, facing us. The owner was waiting on his instructor for his first tailwheel check-out ride. Hoping to save the instructor a long hot walk (so he later said), he called a lineman over to spin the prop. Surely, he felt, he could at least taxi the 100 yards to the FBO.

The "contact" was given and acknowledged, the lineman spun the prop, and the little 65 cranked and idled with a soft topoptika, topoptika barely heard by us in the open hangar. Then the pilot added taxi power to pull ahead. When he started to turn, the plane started to swerve. Now, correcting a minor swerve in a tailwheel airplane presents little difficulty — unless you're attempting to do so by the learn-while-you-swerve method.

The lineman knew the pilot was tailwheel inexperienced, saw he wasn't correcting the swerve and immediately feared for the planes nearby. So he made a running leap and grabbed the outside wing's strut to stop the action. The action didn't stop. In fact the swerve grew into a series of lazy circles with the lineman hanging on and "riding the whip," skater fashion. The airplane made three 360s before the dazed lineman turned loose. (Later, as we were putting it all together, we recalled seeing smoke trailing from the lineman's skidding shoes.)

When the lineman dropped away, the airplane did momentarily straighten out — directly toward the open hangar. Milling about in the wide doorway, we were of divided minds. Some made a dash toward the rolling plane, while the rest of us dodged away from the approaching Juggernaut. When the airplane entered the hangar, reverberating echoes made the soft-chugging taxiing engine sound like something off the wing of a B-29. There was a lot of arm waving and shouted instructions to the pilot, but as he whizzed past, the glazed look in his eyes told me he'd lost interest in the whole affair.

The small Luscombe caromed off the tail section of a Cherokee, whacked the shop's pickup with a wing and threw itself nose first into the hangar's far rear corner. There, among the clatter and clamor of splintering wood and delicate aluminum tearing against steel wall, the little ship fitfully beat itself to pieces.

Well, damage was substantial, but miraculously no one was hurt (although I understand the pilot was never again quite himself).

The point of this whole story, of course, is that we can't safely teach ourselves how to handle a tailwheel airplane. An instructor is needed from the first "contact."

Choosing Your Instructor

Choose your instructor carefully, someone who will be thoroughly familiar with the model you intend to check out. Because in order to let you learn firsthand the landing capabilities of the plane, you must be permitted to go right to the plane's limits. And this means you occasionally test your instructor's ability to make a recovery. Your instructor must know that airplane!

If at all possible, select an instructor with a good sense of humor. Chances are, you'll do some genuinely funny things as you learn to master the machine. Things, for example, like working the elevator exactly out of phase with the bunny hops as you attempt to correct your first bounced landing. (Instructor says, "I got it! I got it!") Or the first landing you make with a foot on one brake. (Instructor says, "Well, at least you know which way it's gonna ground loop.") Having an instructor with a sense of humor aboard lets you share the mirth.

Tailwheels — The Facts

Before you climb aboard with your instructor to start the checkout, let's pinpoint the one great difference between tailwheel and nosewheel airplanes. This difference gives the tailwheeler its ground handling characteristics. Put simply, the main gear of a nosewheel lies *behind* the plane's center of gravity, whereas on a tailwheeler, it lies *ahead* of the center of gravity.

It's necessary that the landing gears be so arranged because a nosewheeler, with its center of weight behind the main wheels, would rest on the ramp with its tail touching the ground and the tailwheeler, with its weight forward, would rest with its nose on the ground (see Figure 19-1).

Tailwheels And Cannonballs

A tailwheel pilot must understand the significance of a center of gravity that lies aft of the main gear. Once you understand this significance, you know what to expect when landing your tailwheeler.

To understand the forces at work, visualize "center of gravity." Rather than think of it as the designer's small cross on a drawing that denotes center of mass, let's visualize it as a great, black, iron cannonball. Load this cannonball in the fuselage ahead of the main gear of a nosewheeler and behind the gear of a tailwheeler. Then let's shove each airplane to get it rolling down the runway with its cannonball aboard. Now, which airplane has the greater tendency to turn end-around?

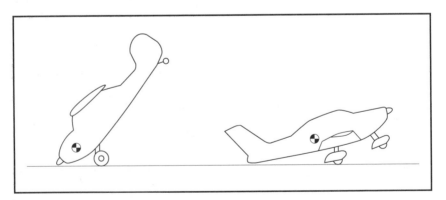

Figure 19-1
A nosewheeler, with the center of gravity aft of the main wheels, would rest with its tail on the ground. A center of gravity ahead of a tailwheeler's gear would put the plane's nose to the ground.

The tailwheeler, naturally, with its center of gravity behind the main wheels. Each small swerve gives the cannonball momentum; the tail tries to overtake the nose. On the other hand, the nosewheeler's center of gravity, ahead of the main wheels, actually tends to straighten out any swerve (see Figure 19-2). In landing a tailwheel airplane, then, you have an important task to perform, one which is not nearly so vital in a nosewheeler. You must try to land with a degree of perfection that prevents a swerve from ever starting. If a swerve should start, you must prevent it from gaining momentum.

Let's see how a tailwheeler's center of gravity invites a swerve, and how the nosewheel design minimizes a swerve during touchdown, rollout, and taxi.

Touchdown

It's important that a tailwheel airplane touch down with a near-perfect crosswind correction and at a precise landing speed. Visualize the cannonball behind the landing gear. If the tailwheeler touches down in a crab angle or while drifting, momentum starts to swing the ball. The same thing happens with a nosewheeler, of course, but with a significant difference. Here, if the plane touches

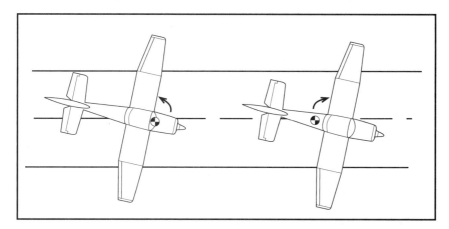

Figure 19-2
A center of gravity that lies ahead of the main wheels tends to stabilize ground handling.

in a crab, the center of gravity ahead of the main wheels tends to bring the nose around straight, and once the nose wheel contacts the runway, it tends to brace the drifting airplane.

Proper touchdown speed is critical to a smooth landing in a tailwheeler. The airplane must dissipate its flying speed as it lands; it must touch down "full stall." This speed translates to the "three point attitude" (all three tires touch at once), which is also the stall attitude of the airplane.

Two undesirable occurrences take place if the tailwheeler touches tail high with flying speed remaining. First, the momentum of the touchdown sends the cannonball (and the tail) hurtling downward. This in turn increases the wing's angle of attack, and with a smidge of flying speed remaining, the airplane lifts off.

Later in your tailwheel checkout, the instructor will have you doing "wheel landings." These landings are useful in gusty conditions where it becomes difficult to exactly time the three point attitude with stalling speed. Here, you literally fly the airplane onto the runway and touch down with a few knots of flying speed remaining and the tail well above the runway. But you'll also be taught a method of preventing the touchdown's momentum from forcing the tail downward to produce an increase in the wing's angle of attack. You'll probably be asked to exert forward stick pressure as the tires touch, to keep the tail high until flying speed is lost.

Since the touchdown attitude (and the resultant touchdown speed) is so important to a tailwheel landing, here's a suggestion: before you start your formal checkout, ride as a passenger in the airplane. Have your pilot taxi you around so the three-point landing attitude is familiar to you. Then ask your instructor to fast-taxi down the runway with the tail high; this to see the "wheel landing" attitude. Finally, take a long, outside look at the three-point attitude. Notice how your ship rests in contact with the ground on the backside of the tires. Carry that mental image — backside of tires — as you land your tail-wheeler.

Rollout

During the rollout, some of your control over that loose cannonball behind the wheels is taken from you, since much of the rudder control is taken from you as you slow down. The "steerable tailwheel" is marginally steerable, and the brakes on most tail-wheelers were obviously designed by a demolition-derby driver who had no intention of stopping anyway. Modern tricycle-gear airplanes, on the other hand, provide good nosewheel steering and disk brakes.

So, during the tailwheeler rollout, make the best use of your remaining control. You may not be able to prevent small swerves from occurring, but alertness and quick actions easily keep them under control. Alertness in this case means keeping your eyes straight ahead and keeping your plane's fuselage lined up with the runway's centerline. If you look inside the cockpit to reach for a knob or switch, even momentarily, a significant swerve is likely. If your runway has no centerline, focus your attention on the far end of the runway during rollout. This gives you a reasonably good straight-line reference.

Quick action to minimize swerves during rollout means anticipating the correction so control pressures are given the instant they are needed. This ability to anticipate isn't hard to learn. It's just developing a feel for the direction the swerve is about to take, and can be related to some childhood games. Did you ever balance on a rail, standing with one foot behind the other? You soon learned to "feel" which way you were about to tip and simply applied body language to prevent it. Where did you "feel" the balance? In your seat. Remember the "slow race" on your bicycle? Who could ride the slowest without falling? Again, the feel in the seat of your pants told you which way to weave the handlebar.

Concentration and the seat of your pants give positive control during rollout.

Taxiing to the Ramp

A normal breeze passes almost unnoticed when you taxi a tricycle plane; the nosewheel acts as a sea anchor when a puff of wind hits the vertical stabilizer. But a tailwheeler often wants to weather vane like a wind sock. The secret here is undiminished vigilance. Plan ahead so that if an upcoming turn places the wind's force against your vertical stabilizer, you can slow your plane and decide if the wind's direction of force calls for less or more turning on your part; learn to use the wind as a partner, not an adversary.

Quartering winds as you taxi are more noticeable without the stabilizing effect of a nosewheel. Proper stick control has the elevator deflected up in a quartering headwind, and down when the wind blows from the rear. Both moves, of course, are to keep the wind from pushing against the elevator's bottom surface. For the same reason, a quartering headwind calls for up aileron in the direction of the wind, whereas a trailing wind requires down aileron held against it.

For more fun, if you're very lucky, you may be too short to see directly over the nose as you taxi. Then you must S-turn as did those pilots of old in their long-legged, high-tired biplanes. S-turns ask you to weave left and stretch your neck right, then weave right and stretch left, all the way to tie-down. And if you meet a modern tricycle-gear airplane taxiing toward you, don't expect the pilot to recognize your plight. Just pull over to the side and let that purring engine, streamlined fuselage, and swept tail scoot past.

There you have it. All that's left now is to rent a tailwheeler, choose an instructor, load your great black cannonball aboard, dust off the seat of your pants, and go back to touch flying's golden age (see Figure 19-3).

Figure 19-3
The Golden Age of flight.

Epilog

As pilots, we share a unique position from which to introduce the values and disciplines of the cockpit to the children around us. And should a young person make known the dream to fly, we must consider forwarding that dream with as much effort, encouragement or sacrifice as we can comfortably provide. Lessons learned at altitude, first hand, will serve that young person as a splendid, lifelong investment of personal excellence. For it's no coincidence that so very many men and women of outstanding achievement have an element of flying in their backgrounds.

Chapter 20

The High Ground

The drowsy summer day was well underway. Cicadas sang, and the aroma of pine wafted across the airport's infield to mix with the perfume of a freshly mowed runway. The arrival's third go-around brought the rural airport hang-arounders to their feet.
They left their makeshift chairs of red Craftsman tool chests and cased Aeroshell and moved as a group from the wooden hangar out into the warm afternoon sunshine.

All noses pointed upward and outward along the strip's departure path. Two hundred horsepower of echoes still bounced through the pine, and beech-covered knolls surrounding the small Smokey Mountain airport that lay hidden within a fold of the Appalachians.

The onlookers caught sight of the streamlined plane banking to downwind for another go. On this one, the pilot cinched his pattern in tight and killed power with a fierce determination the folks on the ground could feel. The gang scurried over to the vantage point by the sock to enjoy the only excitement the sleepy airport ever provided; watching a flatland-trained pilot trying to squeeze a citified-airplane into a short-strip mountain airport.

The sleek retractable sank through base like a wounded U-boat, did a little Stuka dive down short final, and landed with a *whump* that would do any carrier pilot proud. Heavy feet on the brakes sent divots flying from the turf as the bounding plane whisked past the wind sock and swung to a lurching stop alongside the line shack.

Personally, I thought the passenger looked a bit tight around the mouth as she stumbled from the cockpit. But the pilot was a picture of confidence as he bent down to count the wheels, ordered the tanks topped, and went in search of a taxicab.

Rented plane, I thought to myself.

I had a flight on and couldn't stick around to watch the pilot try to track down Bernie, the town's only cabbie. I next saw the pilot two afternoons later. He had returned for departure, passenger in tow (but not following too closely, I noticed). The pilot stuffed the suitcases into the aft hatch and climbed aboard with the passenger. As the pilot fiddled with starting the fuel-injected engine, I saw Gerry, the airport owner, standing nearby, watching. Gerry is a romantic sort; he likes to withhold his help until the last dramatic moment. He didn't make his move until the prop started. Then he stepped alongside and chopped his hands for the pilot to kill the mags.

"Don'tja know you can get into a place you can't get out of?"

Gerry and the pilot then reviewed the plane's performance charts. On landing, the plane needed 1,980 feet — a snug fit for the 2,600-foot mountain strip, but the pilot had made it. The takeoff chart said something worse: with the breezeless midday heat, baggage and topped-off tanks, 2,395 feet. Too tight for safe comfort across the turf runway. If the pilot waited until tomorrow, Gerry explained, the cool morning breeze and defueling to half tanks just might make a takeoff fine — and there was a big municipal airport with plenty of gas only 20 minutes down the valley. Gerry was about to suggest they remain overnight when he noticed the passenger already mounting a search for Bernie...

Pilots trained in the flatlands sometimes feel intimidated when first flying to a mountain destination Yet these airports offer some of the best adventure and satisfaction any light plane can give its pilot.

Whether flying to the sharp Rockies of the west, or the rounded Appalachians of the east, mountain arrivals and departures do require a bit of high-ground expertise. With a few facts in hand and some "pre-mountain training," however, any anxieties quickly melt into an eagerness for the voyage and challenge.

Mountain Arrivals

Gusty Crosswinds

I've stood and watched the wind socks at opposite ends of a mountain runway blowing simultaneously, in opposite directions. Obviously, with all those peaks, ridges, and gullies for the wind to flow over, around, and through, tricky crosswinds are a hallmark of a mountain landing. And many mountain runways are narrow; accuracy counts. Any pilot planning a flight to the high country would be wise to spend a few windy days sharpening skills at the home airport.

Approach Speed and Go-arounds

The unexpectedly high touchdown speed brought about by the high-density altitude has caused many flatland pilots to overshoot. Fly your mountain approach at your normal *indicated* airspeed. But recognize that your *true* airspeed is somewhat higher. This, of course, produces a higher ground speed during the approach and touchdown, which invites an overshoot and requires a longer stopping distance.

By example, the true approach and touchdown speed at a 4,000-foot elevation with an O.A.T. of 80°F will be about 10% greater than at an airport near sea level. To see for yourself what this does to the available landing distance, pick a section of your home runway that duplicates the length of the proposed mountain airport. Then practice some landings from an approach speed 10% faster than your normal, flight-manual airspeed. You'll discover that each five knots of extra speed lengthens your landing distance by about 10%.

Be sure to include some go-arounds, since they are common to mountain approaches. To make these go-arounds realistic, stack the cards against yourself. First, load your airplane with the weight with which you expect to travel. Second, allow only 75% power for your practice go-arounds, to simulate the plane's climb capability at a high elevation.

Mountain Illusions

Many mountain runways may be narrower than those with which you are familiar. And many mountain runways are laid on a slope. Either condition creates an optical illusion during final approach. A narrow runway can make it look like you're too high, possibly tricking you into a too-low approach. If you approach an upsloping runway, it will look like you're too high and may cause you to mistakenly increase your descent. Conversely, a downsloping runway gives the illusion you're too low and invites an overshoot. (The *Airport/Facility Directory* supplies a runway's direction and gradient of slope for preflight research.) All of this means constant reference to your altimeter is critical to a mountain approach.

Mountain Departures

Some mountain airports have a one-way runway; takeoffs are made downhill on the sloping runway. The question might arise at departure: should I take off uphill into the wind, or downhill with the wind at my tail? On a one-way strip there's only one way; you must take off downhill even if downwind.

Let me add that the runway gradient is seldom the real problem here. Almost always it's the terrain at the upcountry end of the runway that stops the whole action. Your wheels may leave the ground when they're supposed to. You may climb after a fashion. But from the wrong end of a one-way strip, you may not be able to climb fast enough to clear the upsloping terrain at the upcountry side of the airport.

Tailwind Performance

Another question might arise: how much tailwind can I accept when departing a one-way airport? Look to your plane's takeoff performance chart for an answer. First, find the no-wind total distance to clear for the prevailing runway conditions. Then apply a rule of thumb: add 20% of that distance for each five knots of tailwind component. Thus, if your plane requires 2,350 feet to achieve a 50-foot altitude for the field elevation, temperature, and loading, it would need at least 3,290 feet with a 10-knot tailwind (plus of course, your usual margin for safety).

Tailwind takeoffs need a lot of room for two reasons. First, with the wind behind you, you use considerable ground run just to get the wings and propeller in "zero wind." Then you need the manual's distance to further accelerate to flying airspeed. Second, once off, the tailwind has you at a higher-than-normal ground speed. You travel the air distance quickly. If, after your rule-of-thumb estimate, you're still in doubt, apply another rule-of-thumb: don't go. Simply delay your takeoff until the wind either shifts or subsides.

Mountain Climbouts

In the mountains, wind can affect safety during the climb-to-altitude phase of your departure. Nearby peaks and ridges may funnel the wind to produce significant turbulence and downdrafts. Expect this turbulence to exist if your airport is within ten miles downwind from the mountain's higher ground. Downdrafts predominate in the flow of this turbulence, and the drafts can be strong enough to seriously affect your climb. Should you encounter a downdraft (noted by a big dip on the VSI) don't get over-worried. These drafts seldom go to the ground; they normally leave the pilot with ample maneuvering room. Simply apply maximum-performance pitch and power until you regain your normal climb. A good rule to follow is this: when surface wind at your airport exceeds 20 knots, postpone your departure until the winds subside; the wind's velocity at mountain-top altitude will be much stronger with even greater turbulence.

Aircraft Capability and Pilot Skill

Your mountain-airport takeoff will be less critical if two facts are in evidence. First, make sure your plane has the performance. A study of the takeoff and climb charts before you even head for the mountains is in order. Compare expected performance against the expected environment as indicated by the sectional chart, weather forecast for the mountain area, and airport data in the *Airport/ Facility Directory*.

Second, your mountain takeoff will be made less critical with pilot experience. If you're a flatland pilot planning to head for the hills, get together with an instructor for some mountain takeoff training before you leave. Prepare for those conditions you'll meet in the high country. On a windy day, learn how to handle your plane on a narrow runway in gusty crosswinds. You and your instructor should load a passenger or cases of engine oil (the line shack will loan them to you) aboard to simulate your expected loading. Remember, weight is critical to mountain departures. You would be wise to limit your useful load to 75% of its maximum allowable. And, if your proposed destination features a one-way strip, be sure to include a practice tailwind takeoff.

Handicap your takeoff to see what you and your plane can deliver on a high-density-altitude departure. Restrict your takeoff power by 50 RPM for each 1,000 feet of field elevation you wish to simulate. Thus, if your engine normally turns 2500 RPM on the takeoff run, restrict power to 2350 RPM to simulate a hot field 3,000 feet higher than your home airport.

Try to imagine a 500-foot ridge two miles out as your plane struggles for altitude. Obviously, you want to conduct this dual instruction from a long runway with no obstacle in sight. And you want to keep your throttle hand limber, just in case the action becomes too uncomfortable.

This simulation will provide realism. But there's a void between *realism* and *reality*. How narrow or how wide that void is, I cannot say with certainty. Therefore, I suggest a final precaution when flying toward that mountainous area. Land at an airport just short of the range. Get together with a local instructor for an hour of refresher training and advice about the mountain terrain you intend to fly through.

Then, with the facts in hand, recent training, and a plane of demonstrated capability, you should have no trouble enjoying the adventures in discovering those airports hidden within the folds of those magnificent mountains.

Chapter 21

Crossing Winds

Imagine — from the rear-seat passenger's point of view — a crosswind landing gone awry. First, there's the impression over the nose and down final that the plane is pointed cockeyed and going to miss the whole runway. Then, if the pilot goofs at touchdown, squalling tires... sickening swerve as best felt from the rear seat... runway edge coming up fast. It's enough to pump squirts of adrenaline from the hardiest passengers' ears and give them a tale to tell around the water cooler for months to come.

The inability to handle crosswinds safely has been a leading producer of lightplane accidents for decades. Not many people get hurt, but even a tattered wing tip is expensive to repair. And plan on the cost of a new automobile if the side load is heavy enough to collapse a gear and put your prop into the runway with sudden stoppage.

The crosswind landing is a complex maneuver to understand and execute. There are many changing forces for the pilot to evaluate and juggle simultaneously, and the extremely high degree of control, coordination, and timing required is seldom matched by any other phase of a normal flight. This means the pilot must use the technique frequently to remain proficient.

However, many pilots are simply unable to fly as often as they wish. And they wisely elect not to fly in crosswinds that could test their ability to handle them. So we have two opposing facts of flight. The first says we must use it or lose it, while the second — the logic of safety — tells us not to use it when it'll do us the most good by testing our skill. It's no wonder our crosswind ability is one of the first pilot skills to get rusty, or that this deficiency remains a major cause of flying accidents.

Let's look at some ways to safely maintain and expand crosswind skill, then "follow through" on the execution of a typical crosswind landing as we review some of the basic concepts and techniques of the maneuver.

Maintaining and Expanding Crosswind Skill

As pilots, we must continually strive to improve our airmanship. Our skills of flight either improve or slowly erode, but they rarely remain unchanged.

Consider these three avenues of recurrent training to hone your crosswind talent: crosswind drills at altitude, solo practice landings in moderate crosswinds, dual instruction in winds beyond your present ability.

Drills at Altitude

An element of crosswind technique troublesome for many pilots is performing the shift from a "crab" used down final, to the crosswind slip used just prior to touchdown. It's no wonder we have trouble developing the control coordination needed here. With each crosswind landing we're exposed to this "shift" for only a few seconds, during which our minds are diverted elsewhere — controlling airspeed, gauging rate of sink, puckering in anticipation that the rapidly approaching runway might smack us. We have neither time nor opportunity to perfect control coordination.

But crosswind drill at altitude provides a method of developing this coordination in relaxed comfort.

Here's how it works: Pick out a long road or similar straight line which lies crosswind. At 2,500 feet above the road, establish a crab-angle that prevents drift. Then, throttle back to let your plane descend along the road at approach speed. Ease from the crab into a crosswind slip, using the road as a runway centerline. You'll have nearly two minutes, completely relaxed, to play with the wind as you make repeated shifts from crab to slip. Level off 1,500 feet above the road, climb back to your starting altitude, reverse direction, then practice with an opposite crosswind.

Many pilots make an important discovery during this drill. They find they've not been using nearly enough opposite rudder during a crosswind slip, a fairly common shortcoming. Try experimenting with twice the rudder pressure you think necessary, and maybe you'll make the discovery, too.

Solo Practice

Every pilot should devote several sessions each year to solo practice. But let me say this right off: if your crosswind skills have already eroded to "unsatisfactory," your first step is clear. After reviewing the basic concepts and techniques, schedule a dual instruction session to bring your skills back to average.

Then, work solo to elevate your skill to above average. When a moderate wind that nears your limit of skill kicks up, head to the airport for some crosswind practice. But heed two cautions. First, prepare yourself by practicing a couple of go-arounds and remain mentally prepared to do so anytime you suspect a bad touchdown might be at hand. (Most crosswind accidents would have been avoided if the pilot made a timely go-around for another try.)

Second, practice when the crosswind exists at a neighboring airport and do your landings there, leaving your home airport with a wind-favored runway. Otherwise, if the wind increases during your solo practice, you may find yourself practicing two hours of go-arounds instead of crosswind landings. When you do encounter a crosswind beyond your ability, it's best not to fight it. Instead, fly to another airport with a wind-favored runway and land there to wait it out.

Elect to use full-stop landings in lieu of touch-and-goes for your practice. A full-stop landing lets you remain focused through rollout, provides taxi time in which to review the landing just made, and allows for an orderly takeoff. A touch-and-go, on the other hand, asks the pilot to slam the nosewheel down, close carb heat, reset flaps and retrim while rolling pell-mell down the runway. The ensuing takeoff is often a dismal affair.

Dual Instruction

The most practical way to elevate your crosswind skill far, far above average is to practice in winds that exceed your present ability. And the only safe way to do this is through dual instruction. It's often difficult to schedule these sessions. Most often you have to wait for brisk winds to occur, then call your instructor for an on-the-spot appointment.

Choose an instructor thoroughly familiar with the make and model you intend to fly. You wish to be allowed to go beyond your ability — right to the edge of safety, but no further. And coaching you through crosswinds that exceed your ability produces some tense moments for the instructor, who *must* know the absolute limits of your plane.

A word of advice: if the plane you fly is one of the complex and heavier retractables, consider first practicing in strong crosswinds with a light trainer type. Then, after you master the technique, try the crosswinds in your more complex airplane. Mooneys, Bonanzas, and the like aren't really meant for the rigors of trial and error as you expand your crosswind skill.

Follow Me Through

Let's review the basic concepts and techniques of crosswind landings by following through a typical arrival. We'll begin as you're turning from base leg to final approach.

Descending Down Final

As you initially turn from base to final, roll out on a crab angle to hold your flight path steady along an extension of the runway's centerline. A typical error when establishing this wind correction is one of overcorrecting. At typical lightplane approach speeds, only about 1° of correction angle is required for each one knot of crosswind component. If the runway centerline shows drift still exists after your initial crab angle, a heading change of only 3 or 4° usually corrects the problem.

You can't continue to crab against the wind all the way to touchdown. Doing so would cause you to land at an angle to the runway, imposing a side load on the gear and likely cause you to lose directional control. So, shift from the crab to the crosswind slip as you cross the fence with touchdown nearing. Some pilots have trouble coordinating ailerons with rudder when slipping to correct a crosswind. They're not bothered so much by the cross-control nature of the maneuver, as they are by not knowing the true functions of the aileron and rudder. The true function of each is simplicity itself. Each control serves a separate task. Ailerons are used to prevent sidewise drift; rudder keeps the plane's fuselage aligned with the runway's center stripes.

When you use ailerons to bank toward the wind —say, to the right for right crosswind — the wing's lift (acting perpendicular to the wing's span) deflects to the right. The force of this deflected lift tugs your plane against the wind. If you don't use enough right bank for the "tugging power" needed, your plane still drifts with the wind. Too much bank, on the other hand, and you actually move sidewise into the wind.

Of course, when you bank to prevent drift, the plane's nose will also turn if you don't do something about it. That's where rudder control fits in. Opposite rudder is simply used to prevent the plane's nose from turning toward the bank and to keep the fuselage aligned with the runway's center stripes.

So, think of your flight controls as performing two separate tasks. Use ailerons for sidewise drift; rudder for center stripe alignment. But how much of each to use? That's easy — if you use one critical visual aid: the center stripes. This visual reference gives you an instant-by-instant evaluation of wind drift and runway alignment — in fact, that's why the stripes are painted there.

Again, picture the final moments of your approach with a right crosswind and with the center stripes in sight. If you start a drift to the left of those stripes, increase aileron. If, on the other hand, you start drifting to the right (against the wind), decrease aileron. And if you see your plane's nose cocked to the right of the stripes, increase "opposite rudder;" to the left, decrease. Use the center stripes to gauge the magnitude of your ailerons and rudder. Crosswind control on short final is as simple as that.

Rounding Out

Roundout, with touchdown imminent, is a time and place for precision crosswind correction — ailerons for drift, rudder for alignment. Don't count on a fixed control deflection to do the job. Be aware that ground speed affects the crosswind's force against your plane — the slower the plane moves, the greater the crosswind's effect. During roundout, you slow from approach speed to touchdown speed, perhaps 20 knots of change; again, the center stripes tell the story.

Also, remember wind is a fickle force — it rarely blows at a constant velocity or direction, and you must stay nimble with ailerons and rudder. At this close point to landing, there's even little value in glancing at the windsock. Several different puffs of wind usually exist between the sock and touchdown zone where exactness counts. But again, the runway center stripes tell you everything you need to know about wind correction on an instant-to-instant basis.

Touching Down

During those moments of touching down, your plane is at its least stable condition. In transition from stable flying machine to stable ground machine, it's most vulnerable to crosswind. Continue to apply aileron and rudder; aileron against drift, rudder for runway alignment.

Most pilots know they're supposed to land on the upwind tire when touching down in a crosswind, but some feel they must then level the wings to bring their raised downwind tire down to the runway. Nothing, however, could be further from the truth. You must hold aileron pressure into the wind as the upwind tire touches, then increase that pressure as your plane further decelerates. Don't worry about that raised tire — it comes down on its own accord when the time is right.

Rolling Out

Again, picture landing with a crosswind blowing from the right. After touchdown and during rollout, the wind pushes against the vertical stabilizer's right side and tries to weathervane the airplane to the right. Maintain right aileron yoke pressure to help you roll straight ahead. With the yoke deflected to the right, the left aileron extends below the wing and digs into the air. The right aileron, of course, lifts and is protected from the onrushing air by the wing's curved upper surface. As the airplane's roll slows, apply more and more control deflection to maintain the left aileron's "digging power." Perfect aileron movement during rollout achieves full control deflection just as the plane rolls to a stop. It's practically impossible to apply too much aileron late in the ground roll.

If you asked me to state just one rule of thumb with which to protect against crosswind landing accidents, I'd say: practice frequently in crosswinds well within your skill level and periodically obtain dual instruction in winds which exceed that level. Stay a student to expand your capabilities.

Chapter 22

Ghost Fields

There's something about operating from a soft or rough field that recalls of things past. Ghosts of deft Wacos and canvas-armored Spads and the pun-chukata-pun-chukata of climbing Kinner radial engines inhabit those flying fields that turn to mush after a spring morning's rain. Our minds allow a population: Charles Lindbergh, Amelia Earhart, Jimmy Doolittle. Others too — nameless, just like ourselves — seeking the simple joy that is flight.

There's reason airstrips with a tendency toward softness are inhabited with ghosts of yesteryear's planes. Those planes were designed with soft fields in mind. Yesterday's high-stepping Travel Airs and Wacos sported tailwheels that held props high and away from danger. Even at taxi speed, the uptilted wings provided lift. And those huge main tires looked like something yanked from the axle of a Model T Ford; they just levered themselves across the ruts with each turn.

Today's airplanes, however, require special techniques for soft or rough airstrips. Small, space-saving wheels are exactly the right size to drop into any rut or soft spot that crosses their paths. And the tricycle gear carries us level, shoving the nosewheel ahead like a plow; the prop always ready to bounce down to the turf.

What we need, then, are techniques to simulate a tailwheel and big tires that lift over the mire.

Into the Soft Field

Even though the soft surface doesn't affect the airplane until it's down, your letdown must anticipate that surface. Descend with a minimum sink rate and slowest safe approach speed. The minimum sink rate delivers a light touchdown that prevents the main gear from sinking into the soft surface. The slowest forward speed reduces the tendency of the plane to pitch downward on landing — a move apt to dip a propeller tip to the soft or rough turf.

Simulating Old Designs

Those old planes achieved a low sink/forward speed approach with a large, highly curved wing area. We can achieve the same results with power and flaps.

You can achieve a minimum sink rate on landing by carrying a small amount of power right through touchdown. (About 1600 RPM is appropriate to many lightplanes.) Deliver the slowest forward speed by extending full flaps and trimming to the minimum approach speed recommended by your plane's manual. (If this information isn't available, apply a rule of thumb: multiply the lower white-arc airspeed by 1.3.)

Pilot Technique

Put your soft-field techniques into play 400 feet above your half-mile, final fix landmark at the plane's normal approach speed and power. Once across your fix, extend the flaps to their final, full position and trim to minimum safe speed. Since you plan to carry some power right through the landing, delay any throttle reduction until further down the glide path. The combination of full flaps, slow speed and normal letdown power should produce a satisfactory initial descent slope.

Down the Final

Midway down the slope, retard your throttle to the desired touchdown setting (about 1600 RPM) and adjust pitch and trim to hold airspeed.

Quickly evaluate your approach path. If your slope is on mark, continue the descent. But if either an undershoot or overshoot appears likely, execute an early go-around for another try. Your plane is flying very slow with full flaps, complicating a last-minute go-around. (Slow speed and go-around power magnifies the left-turning forces; full flaps inhibit the climb away from ground contact while exaggerating upward pitching.) An early abort decision is advisable.

Down the Runway

Leave your throttle "as is" right through touchdown and rollout. Bring the yoke back to the stop with a smooth follow-through. Continue your rollout with full aft yoke. The slightly up-tilted wings will produce some lift even at rollout speed. If possible, keep your throttle setting constant and let the soft ground decelerate the airplane. Decrease flaps to a partial setting that moves them away from prop-blown debris while still producing lift. (Take care your hand moves to the *flap* control, and don't lose sight of the runway ahead or you may swerve.)

Taxiing

Maintain yoke pressure, power, and partial flaps as you turn toward the parking area. Aft yoke and partial power together produce your soft-field taxiing technique. The extra power helps pull through the soft turf and the prop blast across the deflected elevator lessens the nosewheel's drag. If possible, don't stop until you reach firm ground. Plan ahead to avoid the softest or roughest patches.

If you can't avoid these spots, be ready to add power to maintain a constant taxi speed. It's advisable, however, to limit taxi power to 2000 RPM. Higher power across an uncertain surface can produce an erratic taxi that leads to prop or gear damage.

Stuck in the Mud

If you do allow the plane to stop on a soft or rough surface, you may not be able to get it rolling again without help. Should you get stuck, don't try to "gun" the plane out with power while passengers push on struts and wing tips. Somebody is real apt to get hurt, and misdirected shoves on struts or tips can damage either. Your best bet is to go for help and bring back boards, a tow bar, and plenty of extra muscle that knows how to move a plane.

When you reach firmer ground in the tie-down area, throttle back for a normal taxi.

Getting Out

There's a thing to think about before you land: will you be able to get out of that soft field safely? Put four precautions into play: adequate runway length, weight, pilot technique, and fail-safe precautions.

Adequate Runway Length

Soft fields retard takeoff-run acceleration. The extra distance needed to gain flying speed is appreciable; the plane's manual distance contemplates a firm surface. Apply a rule of thumb: don't go into a soft field that doesn't offer at least twice the manual's total-to-clear-obstacles takeoff distance for the departure conditions expected.

Aircraft Weight

Weight is critical to soft-field performance. Each 100 pounds of useful load, by example, can easily add 15% to the takeoff distance from a soft or rough surface. (Remember the surprise on your first solo? Without your instructor's weight on board the plane seemed to leap away from the runway.) Consider a few defensive moves:

1. You may not wish to plan a flight into a known soft field with a heavily loaded aircraft.
2. If, on landing, adequate fuel remains to safely transport you to a nearby paved airport for refueling, you might decide against topping off the tanks at the soft field.
3. Conditions may also suggest you ferry passengers out one by one to a nearby paved airport.

Pilot Technique

You may want to perform takeoff checks while still on the firm ramp area. (Beware your propwash and pedestrians.) Don't, however, attempt to run your checks while taxiing, to do so invites an accident. Taxi out with full aft yoke, partial flaps, and enough power to maintain taxi speed across the soft surface. Taxi through a clearing turn, then keep your plane rolling right into the takeoff run.

Begin your takeoff run with the yoke full aft to lighten the nosewheel load and to produce some lift from the wings. Once the run's speed increases, however, the excess pitch will retard acceleration through both parasite and induced drag. So, relax some of the back pressure as roll speed increases; keep just enough to let the nosewheel skim the surface, This moderately heavy back pressure is also the amount to help lift the main gear across the soft or rough turf. In short, you simulate yesterday's tailwheel rigging and high-stepping wheels.

With good aft yoke, the plane should lift away before you reach normal rotate speed (and the margin between stall speed and flying speed narrows). As the plane lifts off, slightly lower the nose to keep the plane from climbing out of ground effect. (Ground effect is that phenomenon whereby the close proximity of the ground prevents the formation of drag-producing vortices; acceleration is enhanced. Ground effect is useful up to about 12 feet in most light aircraft.)

With the wheels away from the surface and drag reduced, the airspeed will quickly increase to normal rotate speed. Then, pitch to the desired climb speed for a normal departure.

Fail-Safe Precautions

The extra distance required for a safe soft-field departure is both appreciable and unpredictable. We need a fail-safe measure that will stop the action before it might become dangerous, and here's how to get it: First, calculate the manual's total-to-clear-obstacle distance. Since much of the acceleration occurs after liftoff, figure your required distance from that point. If not airborn with that distance remaining, simply abort the takeoff with no harm done.

Practice your soft-field techniques until you're really good. Then plan a ghost flight. Seek out those turf fields which show as hollow magenta symbols. Fly back in time, get the belly of your ship muddy — step into an old dim wooden hangar building, and say hello to a few companionable ghosts (see Figure 22-1).

Chapter Twenty-two

Figure 22-1
There's something about operating from a soft or rough field that recalls of things past.

Part V

Recurrent Training

"If you want to enjoy flying," I said,
"you've got to be good at it."

Richard Bach, *A Gift of Wings*

Chapter 23

Flight Ready

There's a truism in flying which says the safety or hazard of a flight is most often determined by the pilot's preflight efforts, before the wheels ever leave the ground.

There's a segment of preflight preparation that all professionally-oriented pilots must conduct on a continuous, progressive basis — keeping themselves flight-ready in terms of basic pilot skills. This ongoing preflight program must perform two functions: a constant schedule of training to prevent a pilot's attained skill from deteriorating, and it must provide a means whereby the pilot can constantly monitor and evaluate the on-going level of personal pilot skill.

Obviously this preflight preparation can't be accomplished in the minutes before the planned flight begins. A pilot can't simply shelve attained skill and expect it to be flight-ready at some future date. Skill has limited shelf life; it will remain intact only with regular practice.

This segment of preflight preparation is often overlooked by many pilots. Yet it's just as vital to the safety of the flight as is any other part of a pilot's total preflight preparation. A careful pilot, for example, wouldn't ignore a maintenance schedule on the airplane simply because it was once in satisfactory condition. Nor would that pilot eliminate the preflight inspection just because the plane was well maintained. The professionally-oriented pilot feels the same way about attained skill. Just because that skill was once in satisfactory condition, the prudent pilot doesn't ignore the need for a continuing schedule to maintain an adequate level of proficiency. There must also be an "inspection" of pilot proficiency on a continuous basis to ensure a constant state of flight-readiness.

Keeping Skill Preflight-Ready

Basic pilot skills will remain preflight-ready only through a program of regular practice. This is easy to come by if the pilot flies on a daily basis. The facts of recreational flying, however, are most pilots don't fly regularly. Most consider themselves lucky if they get in two or three dozen flights a year. (To parallel the concept, most motorists are competent drivers — they drive nearly every day. But imagine what would happen to their driving skills if they took the car out only two or three dozen times a year.) It's this majority of pilots who most need a definite continuous program that will maintain their skill to a constant preflight readiness. It takes a conscious effort toward such a program, to obtain the maximum benefit from the irregular flights which they do make.

Frequency of flying is much more critical to retention of skill than the hours of flying. The pilot, for instance, who makes a 20-minute flight each week can expect to retain more basic skill than can a pilot making only a single three- or four-hour flight per month. (A weekly "once around the pattern" has merit; the hop possesses all the basic flying elements of the longer flight — from takeoff run, to climbout, to turns, to level off, to cruise, through descent and landing, to roll out.)

A program to maintain a pilot's skill level must be designed to compensate for the average pilot's infrequency of flying. Not only must this program be designed to maintain a pilot's level of skill, it must also provide a means to evaluate those skills on a continuous basis. Pilots don't have such a highly visible gauge against which they can evaluate their flying unless they deliberately create one.

The continuous program of preflight readiness suggested here provides a visible means whereby pilots may constantly evaluate their level of basic skills. It's designed to perform three primary functions:

1. It makes the best possible use of an infrequent flying schedule.
2. It enables pilots to maintain their flying skill even with infrequent flying.
3. It provides a method of continuous evaluation to ensure a constant state of preflight preparedness.

Make Each Flight a Practice Flight

Nearly every flight offers you an opportunity to practice and evaluate your skill. However, this opportunity doesn't come to you uninvited. You must deliberately plan your flight as a series of practice drills. Each drill can be based on the skills needed to perform the different segments of a normal flight, from takeoff to landing. To turn each segment of the flight into a practice drill, you need to do three things.

First, you need to decide the tolerances you're willing to accept as a measure of satisfactory performance for each segment of the flight. These tolerances are usually stated in terms of altitude, heading, and airspeed control.

Then, you need to reduce your tolerances to writing. The tolerances for each segment of the flight, stated on a file card and stuck to the instrument panel, becomes a means of evaluation that can't be easily ignored.

After you've decided on your criteria for satisfactory performance, and reduced this criteria to a visible test of skill, you then endeavor to make your plane perform within the stated tolerances. In this way, you turn each segment of the flight into an individual practice drill.

Here are some thoughts on several segments of a normal flight, and how you can turn each into a valuable drill to ensure your flight-readiness when it's time to fly. The tolerances stated for altitudes, headings, and airspeeds are suggestions only. You must determine for yourself the accuracy you wish to maintain.

Takeoff

Begin your takeoff run from exactly astride the runway centerline to start the flight as perfectly as possible. Keep the nosewheel rolling on the centerline throughout the takeoff run. This requires a touch of right rudder with the initial application of power to counteract the slipstream effect, and an additional application of right rudder to oppose P-factor (the propeller's left-turning tendency) at liftoff. Use the ailerons to correct for any crosswind from the moment the plane starts rolling.

Rotate within three knots of the aircraft manual's recommended liftoff speed. This prevents an excessively fast ground run that's hard to control and imposes undue wear and tear to the plane, or an early liftoff that invites a stall.

Keep your initial climbout directly over the extended centerline. This requires an immediate wind correction angle at liftoff and continued right rudder pressure against the continuing effects of P-factor.

Climb to Altitude

Climb to altitude within three knots of manufacturer's recommended best-rate-of-climb airspeed. This degree of accuracy means you must know exactly how high to hold the nose, relative to the horizon. Proper trimming is essential.

Choose a specific climb heading and maintain that value within 5° on your heading indicator; either adjust rudder trim or hold right rudder against the effects of torque.

Maintain the exact climb power setting recommended by the flight manual. It may be necessary to advance the throttle and re-adjust the fuel mixture at each 500-foot interval in order to maintain a constant manifold pressure.

Level-off from Climb

Lead your level-off from climb by 10 feet for each 100 fpm on the VSI.

Maintain climb power throughout the level-off process and reduce the throttle to cruise power just as the airspeed indicator reaches cruise speed. This assures the best possible acceleration to cruise speed while preventing a loss of altitude during the final moments of the level-off.

Maintain the climb heading within 5° throughout the level-off. This requires you to slowly reduce right rudder pressure as the plane accelerates from climb speed, and climb power is reduced to cruise.

Conclude your level-off process with the plane straight and level within 50 feet of your desired altitude. This isn't difficult to achieve with positive pitch and trim control.

Cruise Flight

For cruise, maintain the exact power setting recommended and maintain the precise fuel flow required of the cruise power setting. Remember that fuel mixture must be re-adjusted with any change in altitude, power, or carburetor heat.

Maintain your selected cruise heading within 5°. If a slight change in heading is needed to re-center the VOR needle, don't arbitrarily turn left or right toward the needle — turn to a specific compass point you feel will do the job.

Maintain your cruising altitude within 50 feet of that desired. This degree of accuracy depends upon a properly trimmed airplane, an awareness of pitch attitude, and a constant power setting. An error in one or more of these three factors can cause a large variance in altitude.

Descent From Cruising Altitude

Plan your letdown to the destination airport as a precision VFR descent. If you have no more than 5,000 feet to lose before you reach the pattern's downwind leg, begin your descent 10 minutes out. (For example, 15 miles for a 90-knot Cessna 152, or 30 miles for a 180-knot Bonanza.) Before you begin to let down, figure the rate of descent that will put you at pattern altitude near your airport. If it's 3,000 feet down to the pattern, for example, peg your VSI on 300 fpm for the 10-minute descent.

If you need to lose 6,000 feet or more, begin your descent 20 minutes out and estimate your rate of descent against that time (about 300 fpm for a 6,000-foot descent, for example, or 500 fpm for 10,000 feet).

When you lower your nose to the desired rate of descent, reduce power to prevent over-revving or excessive speed. Strive to maintain an airspeed within five knots of cruise speed throughout the letdown. (A descent setting of approximately 55% power is reasonable for most light planes. Once you have your VSI captured, you can vary your speed by five knots with each 100 RPM or 1" MP.) Remember, though, manifold pressure increases as you drop through denser air, so adjust the throttle (and mixture) every 1,000 feet.

Choose a specific descent heading and maintain that value within 5°. Use rudder trim or pressure to counteract the right-turning tendency of a descending plane running under reduced power.

Lead your level-off by 20 feet for every 100 fpm on the VSI. At that time, slowly move your plane's nose to level as you smoothly establish cruise power. Find satisfaction in a recovery that levels you within 50 feet of your desired altitude.

Landing

When landing, maintain a pattern altitude within 50 feet of that specified for the airport. On base leg, establish an approach speed within three knots of the manufacturer's recommended approach speed. This degree of precision requires correct trim, the pilot's awareness of pitch attitude, and a smooth hand on the throttle.

Select a landmark on a half-mile final and cross it within 50 feet of 500 feet AGL. With normal headwinds, this will prevent an approach that is either embarrassingly high or dangerously low; only small adjustments of power are needed to put you down right on the mark.

Touch down on the second centerline stripe beyond the numbers. That stripe is normally 120 feet in length and provides a reasonable tolerance for accuracy.

Set your own tolerances for satisfactory performance in all segments of a flight. Each segment then becomes a practice drill to ensure your basic pilot skills will remain preflight-ready. Don't be afraid to set your standards high. It's just as easy to fly with precision as it is to fly without it. There is, after all, a limit to inaccurate flying and it's as easy, for example, to maintain a desired altitude within 40 feet as it is to correct 100 feet to get back on the altitude. It's simply the pilot's individual choice (See Figure 23-1).

Turning each flight into a practice flight provides an easy road to maintained skills. And there's no doubt that our greatest pleasures stem from doing what is both beneficial and fun.

Suggested Tolerances for Segments of Your Flight

Takeoff

Directional Control	Nosewheel on centerline throughout.
Rotate Speed	Within 3 knots of manual's recommendation.
Initial Climbout	Directly over extended centerline.

Climb to Altitude

Airspeed	Within 3 knots of manufacturer's recommended best-rate-of-climb speed.
Heading	Within 5 degrees of that desired.
Power Control	In exact accordance with manual's recommended climb power settings.

Leveloff from Climb

Power Control	Slow reduction to cruise.
Heading	Maintain within 5 degrees of climb heading
Altitude	Recover within 50 feet of desired cruise altitude.
Airspeed	Recover within 3 knots of cruise speed.

Figure 23-1
Set your own tolerances for satisfactory performance in all segments of flight.

Cruise

Power Control   Maintain exact manufacturer's recommendation for percent of power desired, at proper fuel flow.

Heading   Within 5 degrees of that desired.

Altitude   Within 50 feet of that desired.

Descent from Cruise Altitude

Heading   Maintain within 5 degrees of that chosen for descent.

Airspeed   Maintain within 5 knots of cruise speed.

Altitude   Level off within 50 feet of recovery altitude desired.

Landing

Altitude   Pattern altitude within 50 feet.

Airspeed   Establish approach speed within 3 knots of manufacturer's recommendations.

Touchdown   Within the length of a centerline stripe.

Figure 23-1 continued

Chapter 24

Choosing Your Instructor

Learning to fly is no trivial pursuit. Total cost can equal that of buying a new car; effort and study can easily exceed that required of a college semester and the hours expended greatly cuts into your daily living. Anytime we embark on an effort of this magnitude, we'd be well advised to spend some time evaluating what will enhance our success. When learning to fly, as well as obtaining recurrency dual instruction, one important early decision is that of selecting an appropriate flight instructor.

Selection Process

Select your instructor as one of several candidates and choose your candidates carefully. First, if you know some students or pilots, ask for their recommendations. Second, spend some time in the FBO's lobby observing different instructors at work with their students before and after flight. (Try to do this at two or more flight training facilities.) The recommendations of others and your own observations should produce several candidates you'll want to consider.

Once you've narrowed your candidates down to a few likely contenders, let your final selection process follow a three-part program: an interview with the prospective instructor, an in-flight evaluation of instructional capabilities and an assessment of the instructor's teaching environment.

Interviewing

The instructor you finally choose will be your employee. In any walk of life you wouldn't even think of hiring anyone for a position without an interview and a candidate who shows reluctance to an interview should be removed from consideration.

Conduct your interview with open ears to evaluate the candidate's communication skills. Are responses to your questions and comments delivered in a direct, organized and understandable manner? The cockpit will become your classroom, one that's noisy, often uncomfortable, and moves around. Competent communication skills are needed if learning is to occur in this environment.

During the interview, use your eyes as well as your ears. Grooming and appropriate attire do count. The instructor doesn't have to dress fit for a board meeting, but grooming and attire should be neat and appropriate to the job at hand. There tends to be a strong relationship between personal pride and instructional quality.

An important element of the interview asks you to look for a demeanor compatible with your taste and needs. Different students will react differently to various personalities. Some students want their instructor to be all business, for example, while others prefer a friendlier approach. Needs and tastes differ, but there's a match for everyone. The key is this: does the instructor display a manner with which you'll feel comfortable as the two of you work within the stresses of learning to fly? The student and instructor must work as a team if learning is to occur. This teamwork is best bonded in mutual respect.

The interview also allows the prospective instructor to evaluate you as a compatible student. Instructors will only do their best work with students they want to teach. If there's any personal conflict, it's best discovered at the outset.

218

The questions you ask and the comments you offer during the interview will reflect your own specific needs, but try to include a few basic inquiries important to any flight training program:

1. Does the flight instructor hold a ground instructor certificate? This is often an indication of the instructor's attitude toward, and the ability to teach, the academics.

2. Does the instructor normally provide pre- and post-flight briefings? Pre- and post-flight briefings are a must. During a training flight you may have many questions that can't be adequately addressed at the time. Yet these concerns must be answered, and a ground briefing provides the time and the place.

3. Will the instructor advise you of the next lesson's subject, and assign appropriate home study? A good instructor wants a prepared student and prior knowledge promotes efficiency in the cockpit during a lesson. Forewarned students know what to expect and what is expected of them. Students who approach lessons unprepared, however, are often confused during the lesson and learning efficiency suffers.

4. Will the instructor provide two references? Ideally, one reference should come from a current student undergoing flight training; the other from a former student, now a rated pilot. Don't hesitate to call an offered recommendation — pilots usually enjoy discussing their instructors.

If your interview allows time, encourage a conversation of outside interests. This often tells a lot about a person, and you may discover that you have a common interest with the instructor.

By all means verify the instructor's certifications and record-keeping before you conclude your interview. An expired CFI certificate, medical certificate, or ignored training records can jeopardize your logbook endorsements or earned flight hours.

Once your interviews have produced likely candidates, let the instructors demonstrate their teaching skill in the plane.

In-flight Evaluation

An evaluation of a prospective instructor's in-flight teaching ability is an important part of your selection process. Ask each candidate for a short flying lesson on the same maneuver — straight and level flight. By selecting this very basic exercise, you can easily compare each instructor against the others.

You're looking for two essential instructional elements during these flights. First, compare in-flight communication skills. Does the candidate deliver the flight instruction in an understandable manner? Does the information and elements of the maneuver seem to be delivered in a logical sequence?

Second, evaluate the candidate's flying demeanor. Firm decisions must often be made quickly in the cockpit. In your early lessons you won't have the experience to make some of these decisions and must rely on your instructor to do so. Does the candidate's manner and actions inspire confidence? You must have a level of trust in your instructor if learning is to occur.

Chances are, you'll repeat this most basic lesson on straight and level two or three times as you evaluate your candidates, but this isn't wasted time. Repetition of this fundamental maneuver prepares you for the flying yet to come. Most pilot difficulties can be traced right back to the fundamentals.

While in the air with your candidates, compare the makes and models of the training aircraft they use. The different types of aircraft designed for student instruction are all about equal in the long run, but nearly every student claims a preference. Though usually based on personal taste, these preferences are valid. Students seem to do better in a plane they feel "just fits."

Chapter Twenty-four

Teaching Environment

Make evaluation of the training facility where each instructor teaches a part of your selection process. Flight instructors are often a reflection of the FBOs or flying schools where they work, so visit the facility before you begin your dual instruction. A school that holds a vital interest in teaching people to fly has a staff that extends a welcome. They'll exhibit a willingness to show you through the facility, if asked, and are ready to answer your questions.

On your tour, look for the obvious. The premises should appear businesslike and the staff should look energetic, busy, and happy to be working there. Other, more subtle observations will help you evaluate the level of commitment the facility holds toward flight training. Review the sales area set aside for pilot supplies. Are there abundant books and training supplies available? On-the-spot availability is essential.

Check to see if the customer lobby is adequately supplied with both current and recent aviation periodicals. Flying magazines do far more than entertain; they inform, and are your best sources of learning the ever-changing flight procedures. New and helpful products are described and careful comparisons made of the different aircraft available to you. The written experiences of others will often teach you proven techniques to employ as well as pitfalls to avoid. Easy access to the latest information is critical to all pilots.

Ask to see the area set aside for pre- and post-flight briefings; it should be somewhat secluded and provide seating and table space for discussions. At the very least, there should be a blackboard where student and instructor alike can sketch out their ideas and concerns.

Ask some specific questions:

1. Is there a chief flight instructor charged with quality control? A good flying school won't simply depend upon

their instructors to monitor and evaluate their own performance. Additionally, the flight training environment is constantly changing: practice training areas change, regulations change; local hazards change. Someone must be charged with the responsibility to see that all training aircraft returned to the flight line are in proper order. Good flying schools designate a chief flight instructor to coordinate the efforts of the training environment, and to ensure quality control.

2. Does the facility either offer a competent ground school, or provide for this service elsewhere? The academics are important to a student pilot. Adequate aeronautical knowledge is essential to safety and pleasure aloft. There's a lot of new information to learn and many student pilots encounter difficulty when trying to assimilate this knowledge through independent study alone.

3. Does the school schedule periodic checkrides to monitor the student's progress? These checkrides, administered by someone other than the student's regular instructor, promote student confidence and often disclose areas which need improvement.

4. Are solo flights approved and released by a dispatcher capable of evaluating the proposed flight and flying conditions? Many times, you'll have to schedule a solo flight when your instructor isn't there to help you evaluate flight conditions. Weather (which can move in fast) may call for a decision you're not prepared to make.

5. Are the facility's instructors charged with the principle duty to teach flying? Many flight facilities offer charter services, and some operators will pull an instructor from a student in order to fly the more lucrative charter. This often causes a last-minute cancellation of a flying lesson

and two or three such cancellations can seriously dampen a student pilot's motivation, as well as cause a break in the training schedule. If the facility you're considering offers charter service, find out if charter pilots are engaged to fly those trips. If the facility does indeed assign instructors to charter flights, do they make every effort to crew these flights with an instructor not scheduled to teach that day?

6. Finally, walk out to the flight line and look at the training aircraft. Clean planes, free of obviously excessive wear, are important to evaluate a flight instructor's teaching environment.

Give care and thought toward the instructor you choose. Good flight instructors aren't easily forgotten and chances are, your instructor will continue to guide and influence your flying throughout your pilot career. Time expended toward the selection of an appropriate flight instructor is a good, long-term investment. The best success comes from pilots who remain students of the art.

Chapter 25

Pathways to Perfection

There's a certificate or rating to meet the dreams, hopes, and needs of every pilot. Each have their own reasons to pursue the tickets of their choice. As a flight instructor, I have my own reason for encouraging you to keep training. After earning your private pilot certificate, your flying skill will either improve or erode, but it will never remain unchanged. It's your choice.

Of course, we all choose improvement. But you can only make this happen with a program of recurrent training. And the very best way to accomplish this is through the pursuit of additional pilot certificates and ratings — your best pathway to perfection.

Let's discuss these marks of airmanship and just what these certificates and ratings will do for you.

Private Pilot Certificate

Private pilots are the true heroes of aviation. These are the individuals who made the initial personal decision to enter flying, and then carried through with the commitment and sacrifice of time, fortune, and often Olympic effort — many of whom had never touched a plane before the lessons began.

Many who first aspired to the private pilot certificate entered the lessons thinking their final achievement would be learning to manipulate the plane in a prescribed manner to pass a flight test. But early in the game they discovered their real goal — to develop the ability to exercise the ultimate authority granted to a pilot in command and to accept the responsibility for the safe travel of their ship and entrusted passengers. And in learning this authority and these responsibilities, they received one of the remarkable gifts of flight — they learned the sterling values of the cockpit.

These values are all related to the basic truth of flying which simply says: plane and sky grant no special consideration. Whether we walk the earth as good or bad, wise or foolish, poor or rich makes no difference. When we enter the cockpit we leave behind our earthbound differences. We touch the controls as one — a pilot. If our actions are competent, our flying will probably succeed. And if we are incompetent, our flying may likely fail. In short, private pilots have learned a lot about themselves and their potential as they earned their way to the certificate.

Commercial Pilot Certificate

Private pilots enter training for the commercial pilot certificate for one of two basic reasons. Many dream to work the sky as a pilot for pay, while others have no commercial intent. Their only desire is for further, proven excellence. Both are valid reasons for attaining the commercial pilot certificate. Obviously, if you intend to fly for a living, this certificate provides your gateway. After gaining the ticket, you'll then work toward the specific ratings that will qualify you for the job you ultimately desire.

The pilot seeking only excellence, rather than commercial value, is also well served in pursuing the certificate. If the private certificate taught the pilots about themselves, the commercial certificate teaches them about the plane. Much of your in-flight commercial training is devoted to attaining exact performance of selected precision maneuvers. While not as showy as the airshow stunts, these maneuvers demand the same commitment and effort toward excellence the competition aerobatic pilot holds dear. By the time you master these maneuvers, you'll know every nitty-gritty fact of how and why your plane behaves the way it does. And you'll be able to convert that knowledge and skill into the total mastery of your machine.

The flight experience needed to qualify for the commercial pilot certificate is substantial — typically well over 250 hours of total flying time, about 200 of those hours as a command pilot and usually 75 hours or more of rigorous dual instruction.

The academics needed to succeed on the written examination are as substantial as the flight experience. The amount of study equates to a 12 credit-hour senior-level university term and develops aeronautical knowledge far deeper than required of a private pilot in the areas of aerodynamics, weather evaluation, navigation, aircraft operations and aircraft systems.

This depth of aeronautical knowledge is needed by any safe pilot. In reality, a pilot takes only three basic tools to the cockpit: knowledge, skill, and judgement. Of these three, knowledge is paramount. Adequate aeronautical knowledge is the anvil upon which the tools of skill and judgement must forge airmanship. Without adequate knowledge, even the most meticulous skill or keenest judgement has limited potential for success in the air. All too often, the most skillful pilot — who lacks adequate knowledge — directs that fine mechanical skill in the wrong direction. And too often, the most logical thinking pilot — also lacking knowledge — is at a loss without adequate information to base judgement against.

If the FAA demands this high level of skill and knowledge of pilots they certify to carry passengers for hire, why shouldn't the recreational flyer desire the same level of competence for themselves and their friends aboard? The commercial certificate is a desirable goal for even those pilots with no commercial intent.

Once you succeed at earning the certificate, you can truly think of yourself as a professional pilot. And by "professional" I don't mean just a pilot who flies for pay or one who has accumulated thousands of hours aloft. I simply mean a pilot who has made the effort to learn how to deliver the best that pilot and plane, as a team, can perform.

Instrument Rating

The instrument rating teaches the pilot unquestioned discipline. Many pilots enter IFR training with the notion that flight lessons are devoted mainly toward the skill needed to fly the plane accurately by instrument reference. This, however, is not the case. You do learn to fly on the gauges, but that you learn in short order. The main thrust of your flight training hours will be devoted to learning procedures. IFR flying is a highly structured segment of aviation. Every in-flight situation is closely controlled by an exact procedure designed to best meet the needs of that situation.

These procedures are often directed by communications with an air traffic controller and communications themselves are precise. By example, every word in an instrument clearance has its own defined meaning that calls for an exact procedural action by the pilot. (The phrase "cruise 8000," for example, puts into play procedures quite different than the phrase "maintain 8000.") These procedures and communications take time to learn, not only in ground study, but within the cockpit as well. The flight experience usually required to qualify is well over 40 hours of dual, in simulated or actual instrument conditions.

As an instrument pilot on an IFR flight plan, you'll notice a significant change in your relationship with controllers. As a VFR pilot your communications and procedures may sometimes be less than ideal. The controller, sensing limited experience, is prone to work around your difficulties. Indeed, if asked, controllers will hand-deliver you to destination with conversational communications. But as an instrument pilot on an IFR flight plan, those same controllers expect the same competence from you as from the airline captain. Within the IFR system, everyone must be at the right place at the right time, delivering the correct procedure. Your IFR training adequately prepares you to meet these demands and will justify a silent self-award of "well done" after you chock the wheels.

The disciplines of instrument training give rewards that extend beyond IFR operations. The disciplines will effect your VFR flying as well. Shortly after beginning instrument training, you'll likely notice three distinct areas of improvement when you fly VFR: improved radio communications, precise aircraft control, and enhanced navigational ability.

As a recreational pilot, you may not have the opportunity to fly often. This infrequent flying can make a pilot uncomfortable with radio communications. Often this discomfort prevents a pilot from understanding what the controller expects or just what message should be transmitted to the controller.

During your hours aloft as an instrument student, however, you're taught just how to manage a constant stream of communications in a precise manner. Once into the training, any discomfort with VFR communications is a rare occurrence.

Your training develops the skill to accurately fly your plane by instruments. Tolerances for heading, altitude, and airspeed errors are quite small. This instrument precision will carry over into your VFR flying as the gauges support and confirm your visual reference. (Good visual references alone do little to achieve accurate flying. A clear sunny day, for example, does little to hold a precise altitude or heading.) Pilots involved in IFR training shouldn't be surprised to see their VFR flying hold an altitude within 40 feet, a heading within 3° and an airspeed within 2 knots needed to accomplish the maneuver at hand.

The procedures learned during instrument training develop a keen sense of navigation. Precise time and place become a part of your instinct. This carries over to the VFR cockpit; IFR trained pilots rarely wonder exactly where they are.

I strongly recommend pursuing the instrument rating to any pilots who enjoy flying to the dictates of precise, proven procedure and who have a passion for gaining excellence in their flying.

Flight Instructor Certificate

Flight instruction is the top career in aviation. I say this simply because it's so much fun to teach people a skill you know is going to have a dramatic and positive impact on their entire life. As an instructor, you do your very best to bring this about.

Pilots normally seek the rating for one of two reasons: they intend to use the experience and hours to prepare and qualify themselves for a future flying position, or they intend a long-term commitment toward teaching people to fly.

As a flight instructor you'll gain valuable experience that will serve well in any type of flying yet to come. Instructing will allow you to gain a unique element of airmanship — total awareness. Total awareness means the pilot is constantly and simultaneously aware of situations effecting the three basic elements of flight: the environment, the pilot and the plane. By sitting in the right seat, an instructor has the opportunity to observe and evaluate the total picture of situations hour by hour, day by day. Instructors soon develop total awareness, to the degree that they're never caught by surprise in the cockpit. It's a gift that separates the superb pilot from the good pilot. This "feel for flying" will serve you well in any future flying to which you aspire.

A long-term commitment to flight instruction provides a satisfying life in aviation. First, you're constantly flying — you like that. Second, there's variety; no two students are alike and no two flights are alike. There's something going on every minute you're in the cockpit, and most of this time, you're coaxing maximum performance from both plane and pilot.

The flight experience needed to qualify as a CFI are somewhat different from most certificates. First, there are not stated required hours, other than those imposed by the ownership of a commercial pilot certificate. Rather than stating training hours, the certificate requires instruction and satisfactory performance in specified training procedures. The training and the in-flight and oral testing for the certificate is thorough.

If you decide to seek the flight instructor certificate, I offer three suggestions. First, prepare yourself for, then obtain (by written examination), each ground instructor rating. This prepares you to competently guide your students through the academics of the certificate they seek. Also, you must demonstrate your instructing and aeronautical knowledge to the flight examiner who gives you the certification flight test. Showing the examiner an already-earned ground instructor certificate demonstrates your effort and preparation.

Second, if you decide on a CFI certificate as a goal early in your pilot training, approach your flying lessons with a dual mind-set. As your instructor coaches you in a particular maneuver, focus on learning how to fly the maneuver, of course. But if you wish to ultimately become a CFI, let a part of your mind ask: how am I going to teach this maneuver to a student someday. By developing this dual mindset, you can begin to prepare yourself as a flight instructor from the moment you first enter a cockpit.

Finally, if a CFI certificate is a part of your dream, enroll in an FAA-sponsored Flight Instructor Refresher Clinic in your area. (Ask your instructor where and when.) This program is an intensive two or three day clinic designed to keep existing CFI's current on flight instructing methods and procedures. You don't need to be a flight instructor to attend, and you'll be awarded a certificate of completion. The clinic will give you an early insight to the challenges you'll face as a CFI. And by all means, show the certificate of completion to your flight examiner at the time of your certification flight. The certificate is another mark of your preparation and commitment to flight instruction.

Ground Instructor Certificate

The greatest thing about earning the ground instructor certificate is that it doesn't have to cost you. Serious, in-depth self-study does just fine. (Aviation publishers provide a comprehensive study guide, along with a list of recommended texts.) The certificate can be earned by anyone — you don't need to be a flight instructor or hold a commercial pilot certificate. In fact, you can begin working toward it while still a student pilot.

At the conclusion of your study, you must take and pass a very challenging written examination of aeronautical knowledge and teaching skills to obtain your certification. And in the course of study, you have become an extremely knowledgeable pilot.

And why not have some fun with it. Suggest to a flight school that on an appointed evening each week you'll instruct a group of primary students on say aviation weather, regulations, flight theory and the like. You'll even get to sign their logbooks as a certified ground instructor. (If you're looking for a doorway into commercial aviation, know that ground instructors are as scarce as Beech Staggerwings and all good flight schools need one.)

Seaplane Rating

If thoughts of wilderness lakes and sunlit coves stir your blood, the seaplane rating may be the ticket for you. The typical land-trained private pilot requires about 10 hours of instruction. Much attention is given to evaluating water surface, wind, and currents during taxi, takeoff and landing. Simply learning how to dock can be an adventure, and how are you going to perform a simple task like the pre-takeoff engine runup with no brakes to hold?

Airline Transport Pilot Certificate

Is the ATP a realistic goal for the recreation flyer? Most certainly, yes. Do you know that an Airline Transport Pilot certificate is readily available on a single-engine basis? That's right, an affordable single-engine airplane works just fine.

There are two good reasons for pursuing the certificate, depending on the flying hopes you hold. First, if you intend to become a working pilot, the ATP certificate is the finest statement of competence you can give a prospective employer. Second, if your flying holds no commercial intent, the study, experience, and training needed to earn the certificate teaches you most everything you need to know about flying. Just look at the basic flight experience required: You must hold a commercial certificate; 1,500 hours total flight time; 500 hours of cross-country flying; 100 hours of night flight; and 75 hours of actual or simulated instrument flying. And the academics required are just as demanding.

Can the average recreational pilot accomplish the certificate in short-order time? Absolutely not. For most, it will take years. But what a lifetime achievement award with which to cap your career as a pilot.

Is the attainment of an ATP within the capability of the average recreational flyer? Definitely, yes.

If I've discovered anything from an adulthood of instructing it's this: the average student or private pilot holds the potential for greatness. The ATP, or any other certificate or rating I've discussed, is within your reach. It's really a matter of commitment and priority, meeting to create opportunity.

But what about cost? Well... most certificates or ratings equate to the monthly cost of financing a new car. So buy a new set of tires for the old jalopy, keep it another year, and follow the adventure of your path to perfection.

Epilog

Is flying an art or a science? An old, and complex question. And on a moment to moment basis, I'm never quite sure. Maybe, in practical reality, a pilot lives simultaneously in both worlds of science and art. Perhaps we can say science provides the tools of flight, but the art of flying tells us how to best use those tools. Or maybe put another way, science belongs to the plane and sky, art to the self.

Here's a for instance. Let's say we're planning a departure from a country strip with obstacles ahead. So, we turn to the science of the plane's takeoff and climb charts: field elevation, temperature, wind and load, and the chart's factor for a turf surface. It all looks okay.

But it rained last night and the strip's still a bit mushy. Ahha — now, the art of flying. We must apply the art within us to the science of charted numbers to execute the go/no-go decision. And if we do go, our art must plan uncharted safeguards and "outs" to keep us away from harm in the event our decision was the wrong one. Art and science — each partner to the other, together creating airmanship.

Never hesitate to listen to and heed your logic when facing a situation, even if the science of flight says something else. That's your art speaking to you and it's rarely wrong.

I hope these chapters generated flying know-how, and add to your pleasure of plane and sky. My very best wishes for your ever-growing airmanship go with you to any altitude you choose — and now, let's go out and do some flying.

Fat tanks and tailwinds, always,

Ron Fowler

Ron Fowler
Christmas, Florida Winter, 1999

Index

Page numbers for figures are indicated with *f*, e.g. 277*f*

A

mountain airports, 186
nighttime arrivals, 22–24
pilot condition checklist, 50
radio frequencies, 22
short-field landings, 155–57
soft fields, 200–201
time requirements, 47–48
traffic awareness, 9
See also weather minimums,
    personal
pride-induced errors, 44–45
problems, unexpected
    electrical problems, 117
    engine problems, 115–17
    gear failure, 118–19
    general guidelines, 114–15, 119,
        122
    open door, 111–13
proficiency training. *See* flight
    readiness program

R

radar service, communications, 125–
    27
radio frequencies
    communication procedures, 123
    emergency, 108, 114, 122
    logs, 22, 23*f,* 128*f*
    low altitude flying, 108
    preflight planning, 9, 10*f,* 22
    weather information, 130
recovery techniques, stall, 78–79
red zone, 13
rollout techniques
    crosswind landings, 195
    soft field landings, 199
    tailwheelers, 177–78
rotate speed, defined, 57
rough engine procedures, 115–16
rough field. *See* soft field procedures
runaway trim management, 117
runway conditions
    arrival planning, 16–22, 155–57
    mountain airports, 183–85

soft field procedures, 199–200
takeoff/landing distances, 6, 11,
    20
takeoff planning, 57–58, 61–62,
    64, 97

S

Saint Exupery, Antoine de, 101
seaplane ratings, 232
short-field procedures
    approach pattern, 158–59
    glide path assessment, 159–62
    preflight planning, 155–57
    target selection, 157–58
sink rates
    slip techniques, 165
    soft field landings, 198
slipstream effect
    defined, 91
    open cowl hatch procedure, 113
slip techniques, 163–67
slope, runway, 58, 184–85
soft field procedures
    arrival, 198–200
    departure, 200–202
    tailwheeler comparison, 197
spin accidents, 67, 71
stalls
    attitude perception, 73–76
    pilot anxieties, 71–73
    preventing, 76–78, 107
    recovery techniques, 78–79
stress-induced errors, 45–46
strobe lights
    climbouts, 96
    low altitude flying, 107
    low visibility conditions, 134

T

tailwheelers
    aviation tradition, 169
    ground handling characteristics,
        173–75
    instructor selection, 173